Black Madonna

Unlocking the Secret Spiritual Power of the Mother Goddess

© **Copyright 2024 - All rights reserved.**

The content contained within this book may not be reproduced, duplicated, or transmitted without direct written permission from the author or the publisher.

Under no circumstances will any blame or legal responsibility be held against the publisher or author for any damages, reparation, or monetary loss due to the information contained within this book, either directly or indirectly.

Legal Notice:

This book is copyright-protected. It is only for personal use. You cannot amend, distribute, sell, use, quote, or paraphrase any part of the content within this book without the consent of the author or publisher.

Disclaimer Notice:

Please note the information contained within this document is for educational and entertainment purposes only. All effort has been executed to present accurate, up-to-date, reliable, and complete information. No warranties of any kind are declared or implied. Readers acknowledge that the author is not engaging in the rendering of legal, financial, medical, or professional advice. The content within this book has been derived from various sources. Please consult a licensed professional before attempting any techniques outlined in this book.

By reading this document, the reader agrees that under no circumstances is the author responsible for any losses, direct or indirect, that are incurred as a result of the use of the information contained within this document, including, but not limited to, errors, omissions, or inaccuracies.

Your Free Gift
(only available for a limited time)

Thanks for getting this book! If you want to learn more about various spirituality topics, then join Mari Silva's community and get a free guided meditation MP3 for awakening your third eye. This guided meditation mp3 is designed to open and strengthen ones third eye so you can experience a higher state of consciousness. Simply visit the link below the image to get started.

https://spiritualityspot.com/meditation

Or, Scan the QR code!

Table of Contents

INTRODUCTION 1
CHAPTER 1: WHO IS THE BLACK MADONNA? 3
CHAPTER 2: HER SACRED ARTISTRY 12
CHAPTER 3: HER THEMES AND SYMBOLISM 18
CHAPTER 4: HER TRANSFORMATIVE POWER 25
CHAPTER 5: HER RELATION TO MOTHER GODDESSES 37
CHAPTER 6: ESOTERIC INTERPRETATIONS 48
CHAPTER 7: CONNECTING WITH THE BLACK MADONNA 58
CHAPTER 8: HEALING THROUGH THE DIVINE FEMININE 68
CHAPTER 9: HONORING THE MOTHER GODDESS 77
CONCLUSION 85
APPENDIX: LIST OF BLACK MADONNAS 87
HERE'S ANOTHER BOOK BY MARI SILVA THAT YOU MIGHT LIKE 97
YOUR FREE GIFT (ONLY AVAILABLE FOR A LIMITED TIME) 98
REFERENCES 99

Introduction

The Black Madonna is an enigmatic icon. With her warm heart, deep eyes, and dark skin, she draws the hearts of millions across the globe. This being, known for healing many illnesses and emotional pain, transforming many lives, and inspiring peace, is revered and honored by many as a loving Mother Goddess. She welcomes one and all into her fold, fights to protect the people who place their trust in her, and offers her unparalleled wisdom and guidance in all things, great and small.

If you're interested in spirituality, you'll enjoy reading this book. It is packed with ancient wisdom explained in a way that the modern mind can grasp. These pages are an introduction to the Black Madonna, the Dark Mother who nurtures and cares for all. If you are drawn to the symbolism she represents and seek something beyond the usual traditional religious boxes that bind you, the odds are you are about to find everything you've always wanted.

The writing in this book is easy to understand. Typically, esoteric and spiritual matters are written in a language that makes it tough to grasp fundamental concepts, let alone put them to good use in your life. You'll be pleased to find that this book is nothing like that. Whether you've always known about the Black Madonna and have a fine grasp on matters of spirit, or you're just getting your feet wet with the subject, you'll find lots of lovely gems within these pages. The wisdom offered to you is practical, so you know how to take what you learn and use it to transform your life.

Are you ready to receive the love, healing, protection, and guidance you've always sought? Are you prepared to experience true, living spirituality under the loving guidance and instruction of the Black Madonna? Are you eager to know her? Well, your journey begins with the first chapter.

Chapter 1: Who Is the Black Madonna?

You have picked this book because you want to know the Black Madonna. Something deep inside you is stirring, responding to her call. You may feel uncertain about who the Black Madonna is and if she is of any relevance to you. However, by the time you have read this chapter, you will come to know her essence, and should you choose to let her, you will experience her presence in your life in a powerful way. Before shedding light on who she is, you must understand what the Divine Feminine is about.

The Divine Feminine

What is the Divine Feminine about? Divinity expresses itself in masculine and feminine ways. These energies are present in everyone and everything in creation. If you think about it, you can see this duality played out in every facet of life. There's day, and then there's night. You have light, and you also have darkness. There are the concepts of hot and cold, high and low, big and small, order and chaos, and yin and yang.

The Divine Feminine and Divine Masculine supersede the basic concept of gender. Instead, they represent specific traits and archetypes that are very real and observable in your daily life. Regardless of your gender, you carry these two energies within you. What sets you apart from another person is the unique ratio of feminine to masculine energy you express, and even that varies depending on the context you're looking at.

The mental processes you're blessed with are powered by masculine energy, while the feeling processes are the domain of feminine energy. You could think of masculine energy as being direct, moving from the inside to the outside, providing security, and giving of itself. As for feminine energy, it's not a straight line but a circle. The divine feminine energy goes within. It is a force that nurtures one and all, and rather than give, it is receptive. So, where the Divine Masculine is about creating, doing, and acting, the Divine Feminine is about receiving, being, and allowing. This book is about the essence of the Divine Feminine. It doesn't suggest the Divine Masculine has no use. So, the focus will only be on the person who has drawn you to this book.

People who have experienced the power of the Divine Feminine in their lives have nothing to share but positive testimonies of this force in their lives. She is the energy that teaches you to trust, to rest securely in your faith that your desires are accomplished and will manifest exactly when they should and not a moment too soon or too late. She is power. She is love. She is the essence of what it means to be. Everything you do in life stems from the state of simply being. She is a reminder to embody the version of yourself you'd like to be so that you can experience yourself as this person, and life can affirm that this is who you've become.

When you recognize and honor the Divine Feminine, you'll find you live a life free from force. You know you don't have to do too much to attract whatever you desire because you're co-creating with universal forces. You develop an awareness of being one with everything; therefore, you know that you draw whatever your state of being resonates with automatically. The Divine Feminine is the power that drives intuition, helping you know what you need to in inexplicable, and some would say illogical ways. She teaches you to transcend the prison of logic and trust that your every need is sorted even before you realize you have that desire.

Within the Divine Feminine, there's no way you could be desperate. You don't have that needy, pick-me energy. You not only recognize abundance in your life but experience it on a moment-to-moment basis. When you are drowning in self-doubt, you aren't expressing the Divine Feminine. Those lower vibrations are the Wounded Feminine.

However, all wounds can be healed. All you have to do is open yourself up to the feeling of ease. Allow yourself to flow with life, and life will flow through you. How can you allow this energy to bless you? By choosing to trust more, relax more, and receive more. Choose rest over stress.

The Divine Feminine rules life's cycles. Whether it's the different phases of the moon, the rotation of seasons, or the planting and harvesting of crops, she embodies these cycles. If you contemplate them, you'll find that they happen automatically, and these cycles are the embodiment of birth, growth, death, and rebirth. This force connects to the earth and all things of the natural world. She reminds you that you are not separate. There's a connection between everything about you and the world around you. When you understand this, you'll begin to take care of your environment, and that's a good thing.

Meet the Black Madonna

The Black Madonna is the epitome of the Divine Feminine.
https://commons.wikimedia.org/wiki/File:Gorczyn_Black_Madonna_of_Cz%C4%99stochowa.jpg

Now, it's time to answer the question that's been burning in your mind. The Black Madonna is the epitome of the Divine Feminine. She is not fictional. She is a very real presence, so much so that many are drawn to pay honor to her. In Switzerland, there is the Black Madonna of Einsiedeln. Every year, at least 500,000 people beat a path to her door to pay their respects to her. In Spain, the Black Madonna of Montserrat draws at least a million souls who come to thank her for her kindness and grace upon them. Poland's Black Madonna of Częstochowa sees 4 million people each year. In case you wondered, yes, there are even more statues and depictions of this melanated Mary all over the world. She inspires awe. Her power is unmistakable. Once you get to know her, it is impossible for your life to remain the same. You will experience her extraordinary grace and goodness each day.

What is it about the Black Madonna's art that fascinates many and captures their hearts? Is it simply because she's shown to be the Mother of Christ, the savior? Also, how is it that Mary, the mother of God, who has been stereotypically depicted and generally accepted as white in the West, is seen by others as being black? The answer to this mystery can be traced back to the period between the 12th and 14th centuries. During this time, many would devote themselves to Marian cults, in which Mary and Christ were honored. The Catholic Church recognized this and decided to place her at the center of the faith, never mind that ever since 431, she hadn't been recognized as divine, thanks to the Council of Ephesus ruling against that. This woman, who wasn't regarded as important, would become the one people reached out to in prayer, hoping for her healing touch. They knew she could offer them guidance in all their affairs. With time, there would be Marian cults that had depictions of the mother of God with black skin all over Europe. There was a stark difference in her depiction other than the distinction in skin color. The black Mary didn't appear as demure and innocent as the white one. She seemed to be something far more, carrying much more powerful spiritual significance than her Catholic counterpart. It was undeniable to one and all that the Black Madonna was the true Madonna with unquestionable power.

There's some debate about why these depictions of Christ's mother were black. Some historians insist the only reason they're that way is because of layers of incense soot accumulated over the years. They believe the blackness is a result of candles singeing the images and statues gathering grime from being kept underground. Their point is the

Black Madonna was never black at first but only gradually became so. However, that's not accurate. There's evidence to show the people of that period made a deliberate decision to paint her black, and even if she were discolored, they deliberately kept her that way.

It is laughable to suggest that the Black Madonna is a mistake. Marion Woodman and Elinor Dickson are two Jungian theorists who propose that there are two factors that led to the creation and adoption of this benevolent being. Western European Christians had taken it upon themselves to go to war against Muslims because they were concerned about the Muslims taking over the Middle Eastern Holy Land, and they wanted to take back the places that used to be Christian. These wars are known as the Crusades, and as a result of the plundering, Europe would come to discover images and figures of the Black Madonna. Inanna and Isis presented fresh ways to view the archetype of the goddess, and naturally, European artists began depicting the Madonna in the same style. The second factor Woodman and Dickson recognized is the effect of the combination of the adoption of courtly love and the Marian cult. What was that? People became fascinated by the concept of the "idealized woman." Before this time, the white Mary was the representation of that concept. The people needed something to match that, and so the Black Madonna couldn't have come at a better time.

The blackness of this deity makes her important. Many assume darkness has to do with the bad, the unknown, the things lurking in the shadows waiting for a chance to ruin you. However, black had a more generous meaning during the Middle Ages. The difference between black and white wasn't an oversimplification that boiled them down to good and bad. When you consider black from the feminine perspective, you realize it's about more than that. The Black Madonna is the embodiment of the flow of life, which includes death and rebirth. So, death isn't considered a bad thing but necessary for life to continue. The Middle Ages people craved something far deeper and more potent than that offered by the standard Virgin Mary. They wanted a connection with the Goddess, and they got it. The traditional depiction of the Virgin Mary didn't quite work. After all, the only reason she was recognized as a divine being by the Church was to be the token female for a group of men who didn't care much about women or nature. On the flip side, the Black Virgin represents nature and its power to heal one and all. She represents the power of the female, long ignored and downplayed. Where the Virgin Mary is all whiteness and purity, the figure of a doting mother caring for Jesus as a baby, the Black Madonna is the embodiment of the sensuality of womanhood. You can either find her alone or with Jesus in her arms and a face that gives the impression of gravity and dignity. The Black Madonna's fierce independence is the reason many hearts are drawn to her.

The Meaning of Black

The Black Madonna is also called the Dark Mother, the African Mother, or the Black Virgin. She's always black. When she's carrying the baby Jesus, he's depicted as black, too. The Black Madonna has many historical and cultural influences, but her beginnings are African. You could say African traditional and spiritual beliefs have had a strong impact on the major religions practiced across the globe, namely Judaism, Christianity, Islam, and Hinduism. The Black Madonna is a connecting thread, weaving her way through each religion and spiritual tenet. There are various ways in which the black skin of the Black Madonna is significant.

The Divine Feminine: The black skin of the Dark Mother represents the Divine Feminine's essence. This energy contains all things mysterious and deep. It carries the mysteries of life that no mind has grasped yet and which is responsible for keeping one and all alive. It is a reminder of the darkness of the womb from which you and everyone else emerged. This darkness is where all life springs from. Even when planted, seeds are covered in the ground, left to grow in darkness before they spring up to the light. The black skin demonstrates the power of the Divine Feminine to nurture you, transform you into something more, and restore you when you're worn out.

The Process of Creation and the Concept of Fertility: Black is the color of fertility. It is the epitome of riches. Consider, once more, the seeds left in the darkness of the Earth only to bear more life. The Black Madonna's skin is a reminder of the eternal principles of growth and renewal. Allow it to demonstrate that you have the power to create whatever you desire in life, and as long as you trust in that, you will enjoy continuous transformation for the better.

The Power of Embracing Your Shadow Self: No one is all light and goodness. The principle of duality is active even when it comes to how you live your life. The Goddess's black skin encourages you to take a look at your shadow aspect. It tells you that while you may be tempted to run away from your doubts and fears, it is within them you will find healing, and only by facing them can you experience growth in life. So, the African Mother is inviting you to dive into the raging storms within yourself because you will be rewarded for your bravery and willingness to embrace your shadow self.

The Definition of Inclusivity. Where the white Virgin Mary only catered to one group, the Black Madonna is universal. She is no respecter of race or culture, as her grace extends to one and all. Her black skin is the true meaning of inclusivity and a reminder that the Divine Feminine is for one and all, not a select few. She breaks down all barriers and divisions, uniting all of humanity under one umbrella. Africa is the cradle of life, so the Dark Mother's skin is a reminder that she is the original mother of all children of the Earth.

Many People, One Mother

The Dark Mother has undeniable global influence. Many are aware of her miracles and are happy to testify of them, spreading news of who she is and what she has to offer to the souls who put their trust in her. She has many pilgrims devoted to her for good reason. In Algeria, she is Our Lady of Africa. In Côte d'Ivoire, you can find the Black Madonna with Child in the Basilica of Our Lady of Peace in Yamoussoukro. Those from Senegal call her *Notre Dame de la Délivrance*, which means "Our Lady of Deliverance. In Soweto, South Africa, she is simply The Black Madonna.

What about the Philippines? There, she's known as *Nuestra Señora de la Paz y del Buen Viaje de Antipolo,* which means Our Lady of Peace and Good Voyage of Antipolo. They also call her *Nuestra Señora de Guía* (Our Lady of Guidance), *Nuestra Señora de los Desamparados* (Our Lady of the Abandoned), *Nuestra Señora del Buen Suceso* (Our Lady of the Good Event), *Nuestra Señora de Regla* (Our Lady of the Rule), *Nuestra Señora de la Peña de Francia* (Our Lady of Penafrancia), *Nuestra Señora de la Visitación de Piat* (Our Lady of the Visitation of Piat), or *Nuestra Señora de la Salvación* (Our Lady of Salvation). These are only some of the names she goes by in this region, and it's by no means an exhaustive list. You can find her all over the world, from Africa to Asia and Europe to North and South America. That should make it clear she is revered as a mother goddess.

The interesting thing about the Black Madonna's names is that they are containers of her essence. For instance, she is called Our Lady of Deliverance for a reason. On account of her extensive reach across various cultures, countries, and spiritual practices, the Black Madonna is the true embodiment of unity. She is someone who is open to one and all, the true universal figure. Her compassion is available to you regardless of who you may be. She doesn't play games. She's not interested in favoritism. You know that wherever you are in the world, you can access her love.

An interesting thing to note about most religions is how the idea of exclusivity is often present. In the sacred pages of religious texts, you find messages that indicate God has set apart a certain set of people from the rest of the world. It's natural to feel like you don't matter as much as these people if you are not one of them. However, the Black Madonna is the answer to this ostracism, which is unnecessary. The Black Madonna is only interested in the language of the soul, in which everyone is fluent. Whether you cry out to her or whisper what you desire, she's always there to listen and assist you.

Need to walk the path of the Black Madonna? You realize that all souls are equal in her eyes. It doesn't matter what your age, gender, or social status is. She doesn't care about your personal history. She couldn't care less about how much money you have in your bank account or if you're old and wrinkly or young and inexperienced. As long as each time you approach her, you keep an open heart and come from a place of sincerity, you can engage her in a sacred dialogue, and she will respond to you in the way you need.

Keeper of Secrets of Spiritual Power and Transformation

The Black Madonna has secrets that have long eluded many, especially regarding spiritual power or the ability to transform your life into whatever you please. This goddess is strongly connected to ancient traditions where the Divine Feminine was honored. Thanks to these ancient connections, you can turn to her for spiritual knowledge on how to use the power of spirit to create the life of your dreams. This being is a teacher of the process of divine alchemy. Since she is the raw material (or *prima materia*), you need to exercise spiritual power and bring powerful change in life. No one would know better than she how to progress toward enlightenment.

The African Mother is the marriage of light and dark. She shows you how these forces are within you, regardless of whether you've acknowledged it. You can't always be one way or another, so she reminds you there's nothing wrong with that. You have two sides to yourself. If you take her wisdom to heart and embrace both seemingly contradicting sides of yourself, you'll be wiser and better for it.

Whether you seek healing, guidance, protection, or anything else, you can always turn to the Black Madonna, and she will help you. Historically, there have been many stories about her assisting people who are suffering, whether physically or otherwise. She is the embodiment of the process of transformation. You can do everything that you must in order to manifest the life that you desire. However, to ensure you experience as much ease and flow as possible, you should connect with the Black Madonna. If you're wondering if you have the right to connect with this deity, as mentioned before, she does not care about where you are from or who you identify as. As long as you approach her with a sincere heart and a desire to be touched by her grace, you will experience miracles.

Chapter 2: Her Sacred Artistry

The Universality of Art

The beautiful thing about art is that it is not limited by language. That's what makes it such a profound medium for taking abstract concepts and spiritual matters and translating them into things that many can look upon and understand in an instant. There is no better medium of expression than art. Whether it's a sculpture or a painting, everyone can understand the emotions and ideas that a particular work of art conveys. Expressing spiritual concepts using art is the process of taking the intangible and making it real so that you can relate to it on a level you understand. The moment you set your eyes upon a work of art, you create an emotional connection between yourself and that work. What you take away from what you see depends on you.

Art is a universal language heavily reliant upon emotion and imagination. Regardless of which language you speak or where you're from, you have the ability to imagine. You also feel emotions like everyone else. Since art is rooted in these two things, it makes it easy to connect with it on a personal level. That's why when you are looking at a work of art that depicts the Black Madonna, you will experience a deep connection to her.

Art is a mirror, showing how the world has been in the past and what it's like at present. Some people are quick to dismiss art as being unimportant. That would be a big mistake. Within a work of art is the spirit of the time and the place it was made. It represents what people believed and what they valued. So, when you're looking at a visual depiction of the Black Madonna, regardless of what culture or era it's from, you get a sense of how the spiritual lives of the people in those times evolved around this figure.

There is no better way to create the experience of a shared connection than through art. It isn't bound by geography. It isn't restricted by culture. So, everyone gets the chance to connect to the art in their personal way. When you look upon a Black Madonna's depiction or contemplate it, you find yourself connecting with the Divine Feminine. That work of art is a bridge of sorts. It helps connect the profound and the profane, the sacred and the regular.

Artistic Representations of the Black Virgin

For centuries, there have been many depictions of the Black Virgin or Black Madonna worldwide, especially in Latin America and Europe. You'll notice that the images are statues like the Mother Mary with her child Jesus, except that they have dark skin and hair.

The Black Madonna of Montserrat represents hope for those who come before her.
Csiraf, CC BY-SA 3.0 <https://creativecommons.org/licenses/by-sa/3.0>, via Wikimedia Commons: https://commons.wikimedia.org/wiki/File:Black_Madonna.jpg

The Black Madonna of Montserrat is a statue from the 12th century. You can find it at the Benedictine monastery in Catalonia, Montserrat, Spain. This statue is a unique one carved from black wood, and it's one pilgrimage site that many loyal devotees of the Black Madonna love to visit. The Black Madonna of Montserrat represents hope for those who come before her. She promises comfort to those who suffer and need relief from their burdens.

In Częstochowa, within the Jasna Góra Monastery, you'll find the Black Madonna of Częstochowa, a depiction of the Black Virgin and the baby Jesus. The African Mother is painted on wood and then covered in a coating of gold and silver. There is no goddess or divine being more venerated in Poland than the Black Madonna of Częstochowa. For many of the people in Poland, she represents the Polish identity. She also represents the spirit of resistance. Many of the great revolutions that led to a better way of life came about as a result of people willing to resist the status quo. So, for the Polish, their artistic depiction of the Black Madonna embodies this energy.

How about the Black Madonna of Guadalupe? This image is from the 16th century and shows both Mary and Jesus. You can find this at the Basilica of Our Lady of Guadalupe, which is in Mexico City, Mexico. According to legend, this picture appeared miraculously on a cloak. It was a unique cloak made of cactus fiber.

Regardless of her characterization or its location, these representations typically carry a message about who the Black Virgin is. The fact that she is often portrayed as a black woman is a powerful thing to consider. She is the complete antithesis of everything traditional from a Eurocentric view. Since she is artistically depicted as black, this flies in the face of what is considered Christianity. It affirms the worth of everyone on the planet.

If you pay close attention to the artistic depictions of the African Mother, you'll notice she often demonstrates compassion. How? Observe the way she holds Jesus close to her bosom while she looks out at the people with gentle, kind eyes. Those who know the Black Madonna can trust her to serve as their protector and mother at all times. They are certain she is committed to interceding on their behalf. The Black Virgin is also artistically depicted in a way that demonstrates her humble nature and the power she carries. Her clothes are simple, and her expression communicates serenity and peace. Artists will often draw a halo around her, as well as other symbols that represent divinity to remind you that she is holy.

Symbolism in Artistic Depictions of the Black Madonna

Artwork that depicts the Black Virgin uses symbolism to communicate the spiritual essence of this deity. Where the darkness of her skin represents her connection to humanity, the halo around her head represents her connection to divinity. When the Black Virgin is depicted as sitting on a throne with Jesus in her lap, it tells you she is the Mother of God and the Queen of Heaven. There are other depictions of the Black Madonna showing her holding on to the crucified body of Christ. When she is in this particular pose, it demonstrates her compassion for those who suffer.

Sometimes, the Black Virgin is depicted as wearing blue and white robes. The color blue represents grace. Some say it also symbolizes what it means to be pure, in the same way as white does. These colors demonstrate the essence of the Black Madonna.

She may also be seen with certain accessories, such as a crown. The crown is a reminder that she is the Queen of Heaven. When you see a depiction with a scepter in her hand, it reminds you she has authority over life. Did you know even her gestures are symbolic? When she has her hand raised, she's blessing you. When her hands are holding on to her child, Jesus, it represents the energy of nurturing and maternal love. Some depictions of the Black Virgin show her pointing toward you as if inviting you to connect with her energy so you can enjoy her protection and love. These are just a few elements of the different depictions of the Black Madonna in art.

Connecting through Art

At this point, it should be obvious that the depictions of the Black Madonna are not ordinary. They are sacred and powerful tools that can act as portals to connect you to the spiritual world. Whether you decide to look at her art, create some art with her image, or meditate on her images, you can establish a connection to divinity and allow the Divine Feminine to flow freely in your life. You can tap into this by sitting with the art and observing it. The more you contemplate the art, the deeper meaning you will glean from it, which means you have a stronger connection to this deity. You can tell that you have a profound connection with the Black Madonna's art when you sense strong emotions within you.

If you want to express your devotion to the African Mother, you can also create art of her. As you create, you can meditate on what she means to you or what she's done for you. By choosing to create art, you express your spiritual side. The work you create is not ordinary either, as it becomes a portal for you to allow her energy to come through.

Are you uninterested in creating art? There are other ways you can honor and connect with the Black Madonna. For instance, you could meditate on her image. All you have to do is focus fully on her, and when you notice that your mind is wandering, return your attention to her image. As you do this, your thoughts quieten, and your mind feels peaceful. You can then focus on her energy and what she represents. Think about what you would like her to do in your life. Meditating on her image is enough if you are uncertain about what you would like the Black Madonna to do for you. As you do so, you will experience transformation. The Black Madonna knows what you need better than you. She is happy to assist you and bless you. As a bonus, many can testify to gaining spiritual insight when they meditate on her image. They receive guidance regarding specific situations or about their life in general. As a result, they experience transformation. You can experience the same thing.

Stories and Legends

According to legend, the painting of Our Lady of Częstochowa was done by Saint Luke the Evangelist. It is said that this painting has the power to heal and has healed many. Pilgrims flock to the monastery by the hundreds of thousands annually because they hope the Black Madonna will touch them with her healing hands. In 1655, invaders from Sweden had set their sights on the Jasna Góra Monastery. Legend has it that the Black Madonna saved the monastery from these invaders.

In 937, Otto the Great created Magdeburg. He'd wanted the cathedral to have a Benedictine abbey in it. By 1207, The cathedral had to be rebuilt from scratch because it had suffered from a horrible fire incident. According to legend, only one statue remained standing with candles still burning before it, while everything else was reduced to ashes.

What statue was that? The Black Madonna.

The Black Madonna of Guadalupe first revealed herself to a man called Juan Diego in 1531. She gave him very clear instructions to build a church on the Tepeyac hill. Juan made an astonishing discovery about the hill as he noticed that roses bloomed there when it was winter. So, he picked a few of those roses and put them in his cloak. Juan made his way over to the Bishop. When he handed the Bishop the roses, the man of the cloth would notice the face of the Virgin was on the fabric. The cloak still exists, kept safe in the Basilica of Guadalupe.

How about the Black Madonna of Einsiedeln? She is also called Our Lady of Hermits. Why is that? Because it was a hermit who discovered her back in the 9th century. His name was Meinrad. He was so enamored by her grace and goodness that he built her a chapel. Eventually, poor Meinrad would be murdered by robbers who wanted to keep the statue for themselves. What happened after this is a testament to the Black Madonna's justice. Two ravens tailed the murdering robbers. These birds then revealed to the authorities what these men had done to Meinrad, and justice was served. The statue would then be relocated to the monastery. There, people honor her for the protection she offers to travelers and pilgrims. These are just some of the stories and legends surrounding the Black Madonna. Even now, she continues to bless, guide, protect, heal, and nurture those who love her. People know the power they can use to better their lives through artwork representing the African Mother.

Chapter 3: Her Themes and Symbolism

In this chapter, you are going to dive even deeper into the themes and symbolism connected to the sacred Black Madonna. There is so much more to this divine being. There are many rich and complex layers of significance found in her imagery. This chapter is written with the intent of helping you understand those meanings to use in your spiritual practice with her.

The Divine Mother

When the Black Madonna is depicted as the Divine Mother, it resonates strongly with one and all because of the Archetype known as the Mother. Her motherliness shines through as she cradles her baby in her arms or holds on to the crucified body of the Savior, Jesus Christ. There is something deep in the human psyche that desires maternal love. When the chips are down, and things seem to not look great, some call out for their mothers or at least wish they could have her with them. There's a good reason for this.

Motherly energy is nurturing and feels like safety.
https://www.pexels.com/photo/woman-looking-at-toddler-1832097/

Motherly energy is nurturing and feels like safety. The Black Madonna is reminiscent of what it means to have motherly love and comfort. She is there to act as your shield. She is right there with you, and you are never alone, no matter what you're going through. A mother's love is unconditional. The same applies to the Black Madonna's love for you. She has a bond with her child that is unbreakable. You are her child. You are the representation of Jesus in her arms. She is dedicated to keeping you safe at all times.

Does it feel as though life has been terrible for you lately? Turn to the Black Madonna, and she will offer you the comfort you crave. Do you feel lost and need help knowing what the best option to choose in a situation is? You can depend on her motherly wisdom to guide you. Do you chronically feel unsafe no matter what you do? If you surrender to her, she will protect you day and night.

You can connect with her using her artwork. Understand that art is more than just art. It is the crystallization of her energy, which can and will act upon your life if you let it. Often, in depictions of her with her baby or with the crucified Christ, she has eyes full of love. She gazes at you softly, letting you know that she understands you. Her eyes invite you to come to her and find refuge in her arms. They tell you you don't have to go it alone. You can work with her guidance to feel more certainty and safety. Her eyes carry the wisdom of a mother. What mother on earth could possibly top the Divine Mother?

The Light and the Dark

Studying the artwork of the Black Madonna will reveal an interesting interplay of light and darkness. This is no accident. There are layers of meaning woven into the dance of light and darkness. For one thing, the Black Madonna has black skin. This is representative of the divine feminine and how it expresses itself. The blackness is the source of life, helping you to connect you to the power and mysteries of creation. All things that are created come from darkness first. Some people assume that darkness or blackness is a sign of ignorance or something that is not clear. These people couldn't be more wrong. The darkness in the artwork of the Black Madonna is a representation of spiritual insight and profound wisdom. Think of it like looking into a really deep well. At some point, you can no longer see what's at the bottom because of how deep it is. All your eyes can pick up on is blackness, but cleansing, refreshing water is within the well.

In the same way, the human mind can't comprehend fully or grasp the wisdom that the Black Madonna carries. Fortunately, you don't have to understand it fully. You only need to trust her ability to help you with whatever you need.

What about the light from the halo of the Black Madonna? Or the light that surrounds her? This isn't done only for artistic intentions but to represent a powerful spiritual message. When you are experiencing the dark night of the soul, you can count on the Black Virgin to bring you the light of revelation and insight. If you are used to feeling unsure and unclear about your life, you will receive clarity and inspiration by devoting yourself to her. The light aspect of the Black Madonna symbolizes the higher awareness you receive by choosing to walk a spiritual path with her as your guide. Life is complicated. It's not easy to figure out your place in the world or what you should be doing. However, by turning to the Black Madonna, she will guide you through the labyrinth of living. All you have to do is take her hand. Trust that she knows where you should go and it's a good place for you.

When you meditate on the interplay of light and darkness in the artistic depictions of the Black Madonna, you will find a powerful metaphor. Light and darkness represent the potential for you to grow and transform into something more beautiful than you are. These two elements demonstrate that you have the ability to come up through challenges and suffering and experience a better life. The cosmic dance between the two is a reminder of the poet Dinos Christianopoulos's saying, "They tried to bury us, but they didn't know we were seeds." Even if your life feels a little dark right now, by working with the Black Virgin, you will eventually break through the dark soil and into the light.

Another interesting thing about the interplay of light and darkness, as depicted in Black Virgin's artwork, is that there is power in suffering. No, this does not imply she would like you to suffer through life. She asks you to recall that each time you have gone through a challenge, you have been transformed into someone stronger and more resilient than you used to be. She wants you to remember that the trials you're going through are not the end of your story. Those struggles are a necessary part of your life's journey. Think of it like passing gold through fire to refine it so it can shine bright and brilliant. The light and darkness in the artwork of the Black Virgin is a reminder that you can grow, heal, and spiritually evolve when you embrace the lessons of your suffering.

Suffering and Compassion

Her compassion knows no bounds.
https://www.pexels.com/photo/2-person-holding-hands-45842/

A deep analysis of the Black Madonna's artwork will also reveal prominent themes of suffering and compassion. This is especially the case when she is depicted as Mater Dolorosa, also called the Sorrowful Mother. There is a lesson here in how empathy, suffering, and compassion intertwine to create a narrative that inspires one and all. As the Mater Dolorosa, she represents the ancient archetype of the daily suffering humans battle. When life feels like a burden to bear, the Black Madonna is there with you, ready to be your help. She is full of empathy and understands the sorrows that you are experiencing. She desires nothing more than to be there, to wipe your tears away and lift the burden that weighs your back down and makes your shoulders droop. As the Mater Dolorosa, she has tears in her eyes, feeling the sadness, loss, and grief of all humanity.

The African Mother is bonded to you on an emotional level. She doesn't just see you when you're hurting. She feels every single thing you go through. Her compassion knows no bounds. Whenever you're feeling blue, you can look at illustrations of her as the Sorrowful Mother and draw strength and comfort from her. She wants you to know that you are not alone, and she will always be your companion when no one else is there for you.

The Sorrowful Mother loves you unconditionally like any mother would their child. She is willing, eager, and even desperate to reach out to you and take you into her loving arms. People who have experienced horrific events in life can testify to the depth of her love. The Black Virgin isn't some god high up in the sky, far away and removed from your pain. She doesn't just give you a trite statement like, "My ways are far more mysterious than you could ever understand," and expect you to be okay with that. She does everything in her power to make her comfort and solace as real to you as the words on this page.

The archetype of the Mater Dolorosa is a reminder that you can heal, but only when you choose to be compassionate. Most importantly, you must extend this compassion to yourself. Healing can only begin when you accept that you are in pain. It's not easy to admit your suffering. However, if you can face the truth and connect with the Black Virgin, you will find - in her - a space to grieve. You will find the space comforting. You'll realize she understands you more than anyone ever could. She is the one in the world who would never judge you and loves you unconditionally.

You don't have to be or do anything to receive her love. As you show compassion to yourself and allow the Black Virgin to demonstrate her compassion toward you, you will experience healing on every level. Your body will feel better. Your mind will perform better. On top of all that, if there are any emotions that you are struggling with, you will find relief from them. This is the definition of true, complete healing. This is what the Sorrowful Mother offers you.

Healing and Transformation

Another popular way the Black Madonna is portrayed is as the Divine Mother, responsible for healing everyone. When she is present in your life, she may as well be a miracle balm, soothing and healing you in every way. If you want to experience her healing power, you can. Decide that you will surrender to her and trust that she will deliver a satisfying and fulfilling outcome.

The African Mother represents the idea of hope when things are not going well. You can draw strength from her if you feel tired and are unable to continue with whatever you're struggling with. Allow her to fill your heart with hope, and you will be amazed at how you can pick yourself back up and keep going. Her transformational power turns your tiredness into toughness. She takes your weaknesses and turns them into strengths. If you give her all your doubts and fears, she will transform those into certainty and trust. There is no transformer as powerful as the Divine Feminine, the Black Mother herself.

The Divine Mother is the original alchemist. She takes your human experience and upgrades it, helping you discover more of who you are. The more you discover yourself in her, the more resilient you become. When you are on a healing journey and decide to walk with the Black Madonna, you must first be at peace with the things you feel vulnerable about. What terrifies you? What has left you feeling lost and uncertain? Whatever those things are, you must be honest about them.

Why should you acknowledge these things? Accepting how you feel makes room for the Divine Feminine to work her alchemy on you. The truth about your insecurities, doubts, and worries is they are the fuel for the miracle you expect. They are the raw materials that the Divine Mother will craft into the results that you seek. You can allow this change to begin when you surrender to her. It starts from within and works its way outward, so everyone in your life will see that the Mother's touch has truly transformed you.

Revealing the Goddess' Wisdom

Every brush stroke of a painting of the Black Madonna reflects the essence of the Divine Feminine. As you meditate on this art, you will peel back the layers to reveal various aspects of the Mother. The more you discover, the more you become the thing you discover. You are transformed into the image of the Mother, as wise, loving, nurturing, protective, and creative as she.

Look at all artwork depicting the Divine feminine as the Black Madonna through these lenses. As you do, you will discover the artwork is far more than simple artistic expression. You will learn that the figure of the Black Madonna is a deep well full of spiritual guidance and insight. You will experience and express her uncommon wisdom.

The more you allow yourself to dwell on the Black Madonna, the more you realize she is not your regular external deity. No one will be able to convince you otherwise. You will have experiences that show she is with you all the time. You carry her in the depths of your soul. You can't be separated from her. You may, at times, feel as if she is distant, but that is because you have closed your eyes to her presence in your life. As the Divine Mother, she can't abandon her own. You are one of hers, so whenever you feel alone or as if she isn't there, remember this.

By allowing yourself to soak up the insights you get from spending time in reflection and meditation on the Black Mother, you will discover your purpose. She is an endlessly flowing river of inspiration that you can draw from to your heart's content. Through her symbology, themes, and artwork, you'll discover that the Black Virgin is the one you have been searching for all your life.

Chapter 4: Her Transformative Power

Before understanding the transformative power of the Black Virgin, it is essential to explain what it means to be transformed in spiritual and personal contexts. When you experience transformation, you notice that your life has permanently changed in an observable way. The transformation you experience affects the way you perceive the world. You come to think about life differently. You discover an aspect of yourself of which you may have been unaware until the point you changed. In the past, you may have assumed that you had a firm grasp of who you are and what you want in life. However, when you experience the power of spiritual transformation, all the things you thought you knew fly right out the window. You feel a much deeper sense of purpose than ever before. You are connected to something greater than you. Put simply, you have grown.

WISDOM

FEELING

Your metamorphosis can happen in the twinkling of an eye or over a period of time.
https://pixabay.com/illustrations/wisdom-power-vision-feeling-mind-666135/

    The question is, what exactly triggers this profound transformation? You may have had a series of experiences that caused you to see things differently. Transformation may be a result of a personal crisis. Perhaps your spiritual practices paid off, and you experienced an awakening. Or you may have been dedicated to developing your life. Whatever the case may be, your metamorphosis can happen in the twinkling of an eye or over a period of time. This change touches every aspect of your life. Your thought patterns change. Your emotional baseline changes, too. Even your body can reflect the changes that you have undergone spiritually. It's not a stretch for that to happen because, after all, everything in life springs from the spiritual first.

Inner Alchemy

Inner alchemy involves learning how to change yourself on the inside so that your exterior world transforms along with you. In the original sense of the word, alchemy is about converting lead into gold. In the context of self-transformation, it is taking your lower nature and elevating it.

As you experience different obstacles and challenges in life, you are given the opportunity to deal with your shadows. Choose to be courageous when you encounter these occurrences. Why? By deciding you will not run away from your shadows, you have a chance to heal your wounds. When you experience deep healing, it leads to inner alchemy. You let go of everything that does not serve you. As a result, you create space in your life for your authentic self to shine.

The transformation process involves bringing together the different aspects of yourself to create a more cohesive being. As you experience the inner spiritual transformation, you learn and grow. Most people live from the Divine Masculine energy and completely neglect the Divine Feminine. However, you have chosen to read this book. By implication, you are learning to integrate both your masculine and feminine sides to achieve wholeness. This is the goal of transformation.

The Black Madonna can help you become more conscious of how you express yourself. She shows you the patterns of behavior that don't serve you. She can show you how you've been holding on to negative emotions and how to release them to become the person you are destined to be. What are some of the ways that the inner alchemical process plays out in your life?

Purification: Whenever you lose someone or something dear to you or experience betrayal, you are bombarded with a range of negative emotions. These emotions make it difficult to see the good within that experience. Your mind is clouded by anger. Your heart is weighed down by sadness. There is a sickening feeling in your gut that makes you resent the person who betrayed you or curse life for taking away what you held dear. It is natural to experience these emotions, so do not beat yourself up for not being able to help how you feel. The trouble comes when you don't let go of the negative emotions after acknowledging them. If you hold on too long, they become toxic. How do you purify yourself from this poison? There's no better person to help you with the process than the Black Virgin.

Refinement: Give the African Mother free rein to transform your life. You'll discover the trials you deal with can reveal your talents and skills, some of which you had no idea you had. When she walks you through a challenge by taking your hand and giving you courage, the onus is on you to discover your talents and practice to refine them. For instance, your challenge may be that you lost a good-paying job. You feel done for. This circumstance, however, may lead you to discover you are an excellent public speaker. You find you have a way with words. When the Divine Mother inspires you to use that gift, and you do, people begin to gravitate toward you. They want to learn from you. They're happy to pay to hear you speak. You find opportunities that allow you to express these talents even more. You could find yourself in a line of work far more fulfilling than what you lost. This is just one example of how the Black Madonna can help you.

The Black Madonna: A Catalyst for Change

The archetype of the Black Madonna is the best representation of transformation. She is the embodiment of healing and self-realization. This deity is the representation of nature's dark side. She is the depiction of the unconscious mind and the expression of the feminine principle, unfiltered and unrefined. In her hallowed position as the Mother of everyone, she possesses the power to transform your life and heal you in every way you need. When you invoke the Black Madonna, you draw upon the power of the Divine Feminine, and this power is what transforms your life. How does she help you with your inner alchemy? How does the Black Virgin serve as the catalyst for you to realize your true self and heal?

She Gives You the Courage to Face Your Shadows. The first thing the Black Madonna does is to make you aware of your shadow aspect. It is impossible to heal this part of yourself if you don't know it exists to begin with. As her light illuminates your life, you'll discover the dark parts of your psyche and learn what needs to be integrated and healed. These are the parts of yourself you've discarded because the world didn't approve of them. The moment you become aware of your shadow aspect, she helps you learn acceptance. There is a misguided belief that your shadow is something to be repressed or completely ignored. For this reason, many people live a half-life. They literally discard a part of themselves and wonder why they don't feel fulfilled. The Black Virgin helps you accept everything that is you and understand that regardless of your shadow, you are worthy of being loved. The moment you accept her proposal to be at peace with your shadow, you can transform it. She gives you the strength and the courage to bring your wounds to light and heal them. Then, you can integrate your shadow and become whole.

The Black Madonna Can Help You Live a Life of Authenticity. One of the ways in which this deity can encourage you to be yourself is to accept your vulnerability. You see, her black skin reflects the fact that you are human. It is a reminder that you struggle just like everyone else. In no way are you alone on your journey. So, there is no reason you should be afraid of your vulnerabilities because everyone has them. If you heed her call to acknowledge that you have vulnerabilities, you can begin to live an authentic life. By working with her, you discover your core values. These values will influence your choices in life and help you live authentically.

She Connects You with Your Empathetic, Compassionate Self. Devotees of the Black Virgin can attest that they have more compassion and empathy than before they found her. With her presence in your life, you'll experience the same. You'll realize that everyone has struggles, just as you do. Your empathy grows. Your interactions with the people in your life will become much more meaningful. Why? You deal with others with an open heart, realizing everyone has a burden. So, you treat them a little more kindly, and they give that energy back to you and direct it to others. The world could certainly use a lot more kindness.

With the Black Virgin, You Can Finally Find Your Purpose. If you honor the Black Madonna and bring her into every aspect of your life, she will show you your purpose. Could you use some inspiration about what to do with your life? Surrender your affairs to the Black Madonna. It is inevitable that once you do this, you will have a much deeper understanding of why you came to Earth. The more time you spend contemplating the Black Madonna's essence, the more you will feel reassured. Each day, you'll be more certain about your journey, trusting that it is leading you to the perfect end. She is asking you right now to make a bold choice. She wants you to respond to the call of destiny rather than ignore it because you think that's the safer bet. Even if you feel terrified, you can draw strength from her.

The Power and Impact of the Black Madonna on Your Life

The Black Madonna is the quintessential intercessor. She acts as the middle person between heaven and earth. Whenever you desire something from the spirit world, whether blessing, direction, healing, or wisdom, you can reach out to the Black Madonna and trust that she will deliver on those things. Allow the Black Madonna to play intercessor on your behalf. As you do, you will feel peace that matches nothing else you've ever known. You have someone who can advocate for you and plead your case whenever you are in need. You no longer feel alone by placing your faith fully in the Black Madonna. Once upon a time, you may have been gripped by despair. Now, you know you are always safe.

How can you tell that the Black Mother is interceding on your behalf? You will notice a sense of well-being. Your heart floods with optimism even when you can't see a logical reason to hope. It's as if she pours strength into your spirit. You counter adversity with joy. So, when dealing with a crisis, make it a habit to turn to the Black Madonna.

The Black Virgin has protective powers that affect every aspect of your life when you allow her to be a part of it. Nothing and no one can give you the sense of security that she does. The security she offers is not financial. It does not come in the form of advanced home security systems. She offers you divine security, which is over and above everything else. When you are at your most vulnerable and uncertain, and you worry about who may take advantage of you, she will take care of you.

The Black Virgin protects and provides for every one of her devotees. You can rest in her loving, protective arms in this world full of obstacles and uncertainties. She offers the peace that surpasses all understanding. Are you prone to anxiety? Do you find yourself stressed out all the time? Do you wish you could relax more? In that case, it's about time you asked the Black Madonna to handle your affairs. Once you surrender to her like this, you will handle all the tribulations and trials of life with ease and grace. It wouldn't matter to you if the world were on fire. You would know that amid the chaos, you can find peace with the Mother.

Another power the Black Virgin has is the ability to help you find inner strength. She is a reminder that you can be strong when handling the challenges life throws your way. Some people mistake strength for being aggressive and brash. Often, this is only a show of strength rather than the real deal. It is an illusion meant to hide or camouflage insecurities. What the Black Madonna offers you is more. She shows you true strength, which is a force that endures. It may be quiet, but it is powerful. There isn't a single obstacle that could withstand the strength of the Madonna within you. When you ask her to strengthen you, your doubts and fears may still be there, but you deal with them more confidently. You approach them with tenacity. Sure, you may be in the middle of the most troubling of storms. However, you know you have an indomitable spirit in you in the form of the Black Madonna.

The strength that the Black Virgin offers you is one that you can use in every aspect of life, whether professional or personal. You can use her strength to help you deal with challenging projects with confidence and panache. Are there certain complications and complexities along the path of advancing in your career? Ask her to fill you with her strength. Do you struggle with being authentic and expressing yourself in your personal relationships? She can help you so your emotions and thoughts flow honestly. You'll have no more qualms dealing with conflicts head-on and in the most effective way possible. Whatever your dreams may be, you are no longer timid about making them happen. The Black Madonna's strength encourages you to take risks you ordinarily wouldn't. By trusting in her, your gamble pays off.

Inspiring Spiritual Change

Healing and Letting Go: One thing about the Black Madonna is that she makes it clear it's okay to accept the parts of your life you struggle with. Since everyone has some baggage, she reminds you to avoid letting those things wear you down. Are you serious about growing spiritually? Consider whether you're holding on to old grudges. If you find it tough to bring any to mind, she will remind you of what you have repressed. When you discover these things, you'll see it is essential to let them go. There is no way to progress in your spiritual life when all that negativity weighs you down.

The Divine Feminine is a beacon of light. She shines brightly to show you how to release all the burdens that hold you down. No, she isn't asking you to pretend like your past never happened. If you attempt to lie to yourself about your past, you hold yourself back. Instead, own up to it. When you surrender to her guidance, she will help you understand why you went through what you did. This will be instrumental in helping you release the pain so you can grow. When you realize you no longer have to hold on to the hurt and anger, your life turns around spiritually. This is the gift that the Black Madonna offers you, should you choose to accept it.

Conquering Fear: Fear is another thing that can hold you back from spiritual transformation and growth. It's something every human has to contend with. For all the advancements that have been made in science and technology, humanity has yet to crack the code on how to put the kibosh on fear. So, thinking about how to avoid it or totally kill it in your life is unrealistic. There is, however, a solution. You can hand over your fears to the Black Madonna, and she will help you overcome them. It's not like she's going to conduct a spiritual lobotomy that makes it impossible for you to feel fear. Rather, she invites you to face them head-on. It's a daunting thing to do, but if you trust her, you will discover you've always had the courage within you to handle fear.

You can't make spiritual advancements without overcoming fear. Fear is a restrictive energy. It holds you captive. It keeps you from having access to the wonderful opportunities that come your way. Just when you're about to take a leap of faith and do something that would improve your life, fear reminds you of the countless times you failed in the past. So let her help you with that. You're never alone. There's no better companion than the African Mother on your journey. Driven by her power and mystery, you will find the courage to handle everything that gives you nightmares. You see, the Dark Virgin's essence transcends everything you can imagine. Anxiety, worry, fear, and doubt cower in her presence.

Creative Expression: Do you find it difficult to develop new ideas? Are you experiencing creative blocks? Did you know the Mother is the best person to help you? Your mother encourages you to trust yourself and your abilities. The Black Madonna does the same thing. She goes a step further, offering you ideas out of this world. The Divine Feminine is a creative force. Remember, it is out of the darkness that all of life emerged. This darkness is embodied in the Black Madonna's dark skin. She serves as a reminder that you, too, can create at every point in time.

Something about acknowledging the Black Madonna's presence in your life makes it possible for you to use your imagination in ways you never thought possible. When you hit a block in your creative work, you are often gripped by fear and a desire to be perfect. By meditating upon the Black Madonna, you receive a reminder from her that you don't need to get it right. You only need to get it done. She also reminds you to check in with yourself to be certain that you are creating what you want to versus what you think others would prefer.

If you want to feel her creative power and action the next time you do some work, consider invoking her presence first. You'll notice that you're taking more risks and having fun expressing yourself authentically. Creation is a deeply spiritual act. It doesn't matter if you're trying to create a feeling within you or a work of art outside of you. You could creatively visualize something in your mind or pour it out onto canvas. Either way, this is a spiritual process. The more you create, the more you are spiritually transformed. You allow her energy to flow through you powerfully, and this will affect every aspect of your life. As you create, you move beyond the ordinary. You translate your inner experiences through your work of art in the most profound and unique ways.

Inspiring Stories

Lisa's Story: Lisa is a very talented artist, but the problem is she never let anyone know it. She was very afraid of being criticized, and because she didn't want to be judged for her art, she never expressed herself how she wanted. Her need for conformity and acceptance would eventually become so bad that it would morph into a desire for perfectionism. Each time she put her paintbrush to her canvas, she could feel the roar of many voices taunting her, even though those voices didn't actually exist. For many years, she remained in her comfort zone and would find that the thing she used to enjoy was no longer fulfilling.

Things would change one day when she found herself visiting a Black Madonna shrine. The first thing she noticed about the shrine was its aura; it felt divine and serene. She would have told you it felt like stepping into an entirely different world if you had asked her. She fixed her eyes on the Black Madonna's striking image and suddenly desired to learn more about her. So, when she returned home, she dove into the topic of the Black Madonna, reading everything she could. She didn't even notice when she fell asleep while researching on the couch.

It turned out this was the intention of the deity. Lisa dreamed of her. The Dark Virgin told her, "Your voice is powerful and unique. Your hands have been blessed to create wondrous works. It is time for you to allow yourself to be as great as you are." Lisa woke up from that dream with the feeling that it was no ordinary dream. she would describe it as being "more real than real life." With a new fire burning passionately in her heart, Lisa went to her studio and immediately got to work. The self-doubt that usually plagued her was no longer there. She dipped her brush into bold and daring colors, creating to her heart's content. The first piece she created after the Black Madonna's vision was unlike anything she'd ever done. She was no longer afraid to put herself out there. Since having that dream, her artistic life has never been the same, both in terms of inspiration and acknowledgment from others.

Michael's Story: Michael had a terrible, traumatic childhood. He could remember some of it while he repressed other memories deep into his subconscious. One thing remained undeniable: Michael could feel the weight of all his emotional scars. The trauma tainted everything he did. Imagine having heavy chains around your neck and ankles for over thirty years. He didn't realize he had a date with destiny, specifically with the Black Madonna. On a whim, he decided to accompany a friend on a Black Madonna pilgrimage, even though he thought it was all hogwash. He was only going for the experience to see how this deity deeply enamored others.

Once he arrived, the skeptic in Michael piped up, saying that the people there were a cult. He was about to voice this thought to his friend when he felt a heavy sensation on his chest; without understanding how or why, he felt an intense desire to kneel on the floor. So, he knelt. Yet it was as if the ground was beckoning him, and he couldn't resist. So, he laid down flat. He felt a sense of peace wash over him, the like of which he had never experienced before. The serenity was so great that he wept long and loud. When he would eventually come out of it, he sat for hours in contemplation while the tears continued to flow down his face silently. He had felt the comforting, loving presence of the Black Madonna. He turned to his friend and said, "So, this is what it feels like to be safe?" His friend said nothing but squeezed his hand in comfort and support.

Over the coming days and weeks, Michael would eventually find himself releasing repressed emotions and traumatic memories. It was a challenging process. However, it clearly led to his spiritual transformation. Now, Michael is the sort of man who springs out of bed in the morning as though he's happy to take the day on. There's a lightness in his step that was not there before. He has an easy way about him and is quick to smile. This is the transformative healing power of the Black Madonna in action.

Emily's Story: Emily used to be beset with anxiety and stress. It was the reality of her everyday life. She never had a moment to breathe, and when she did, she somehow would find something to fill it with. The thought of sitting still and relaxing made her extremely anxious, to the point where she would bite her nails to the quick. Yet she knew she couldn't stay busy because she was burning out. She knew that her relentless pursuit of perfection could not be sustained and that, at some point, she may burn out permanently. Yet she had no idea how to stop being the way she was.

One day, while in the library researching for work, she felt the calling to take a stroll into the esoteric section. Interestingly, Emily was one of those people you would call a realist. In other words, she didn't care much for religious or spiritual matters. The way Emily saw it, if it was something you couldn't observe with your physical senses, it was not real and did not deserve attention. Imagine her shock and wonder as she found her feet wandering into that aisle of books. She stumbled upon a book about the Black Madonna, and it was as if a voice inside her piped up, saying, "Take that one." So, she took a chance and obeyed.

Emily devoured the book in a matter of hours. She was so enamored by it that she took it home and would reread it. The next day, she did something she had never done her whole life. She called her workplace and told them she would not be available for the next week. According to her, after making that phone call, she felt a peace she had never experienced. She fixed herself a nice cup of tea and sat by her window, looking outside, doing nothing.

Finally, Emily had learned, thanks to the Black Madonna, that her sense of self-worth was not connected to the things she did or accomplished in life. Emily would discover that she's worthy just because – and for no other reason. Her existence alone is a testament to her worthiness. From that point on, Emily was never the same. She had learned how to let go and trust. Interestingly enough, her career took a turn for the better as she decided to rest more and stop to smell the roses more often.

These are only three stories of many demonstrating how the Black Madonna can improve your life on every level. She wants to mother you. She wants to be your friend, to guide and help you. She wants you to know right now that things can be better than you may have imagined or experienced. There is not one thing about you that would exclude you from receiving her blessings and protection. So, take a moment to think about every aspect of your life. Where might you benefit the most from allowing her to have her way with you?

Would you like to develop your spiritual life? Are you tired of seeking for your purpose? Do you wish you could have guidance at every turn? How nice would it be to go through each day knowing you are not alone? What would it be like to live life carefree and trusting as a child does? How great would it be to know you have endless creativity flowing to and through you? Can you imagine what it would be like to have every need met even before you realize you need something?

How freeing is it to know that you can confidently make your choices and trust that the outcomes will be handled by a being who knows all and sees all? How wonderful would it be to find that the relationships you assumed were destroyed forever are now back and better than in the past? Can you picture what it would be like to trust that no matter how it seems, things are always working out for you? What would it be like to know that you have a divine being who rigs life in your favor because she loves you so dearly? What if you could live your life and accomplish far more by resting and trusting than going out to struggle for what you want? All of this is possible if you allow the Black Madonna to be there for you and with you all the way, every day.

However, the Black Madonna does not force herself on you. That would be against the nature of the Divine Feminine. So, right now, she's setting before you an open invitation. It's up to you whether you take it or not. If you want to experience love and power in your life, you have to extend your hand and accept the help she offers. You may find it terrifying. You may feel some doubt or fear. However, you can still accept her help despite those feelings.

Chapter 5: Her Relation to Mother Goddesses

Did you know that the Black Madonna has connections to Mother Goddesses? She is, after all, the embodiment of motherhood. In this chapter, you'll learn about her connection to the Mother Goddesses across various traditions and cultures. You'll see how she's connected to Isis, Ceres, Cybele, Artemis, Kali, and other goddesses from before Christianity. By looking at the Black Madonna through the lenses of other goddesses who embodied motherhood, you will have an even deeper understanding of what it means to be loved and cherished by the Black Virgin. You will comprehend the different aspects of motherhood and how they can all be found within this one being.

Isis

Another attribute of this goddess loved by one and all is she is a mother, making her a role model for many women.

https://commons.wikimedia.org/wiki/File:Egyptian_-_Isis_with_Horus_the_Child_-_Walters_54416_-_Three_Quarter_Right.jpg

Of the many goddesses of ancient Egypt, Isis is one of the most important. Interestingly enough, she used to be obscure because she didn't have temples of her own. However, as the dynastic age continued, more and more people began to acknowledge that she was important. She had a lot of devotees from ancient Egypt and ancient Rome to Afghanistan and England. Even in this day and age, she is honored by pagans.

Isis has a powerful connection with the dead, as she was considered central to all burial rights. She is also strongly connected to life because she is known to be a magical healer who helps the sick and even restores the dead to life. Another attribute of this goddess loved by one and all is she is a mother, making her a role model for many women.

The Egyptian kingship was aware that Isis was important and worth revering. She is depicted as a woman who wears a sheath dress. She also has the horns of a cow on her head, as well as a solar disk. Some of the artistic depictions will also include a hieroglyphic throne. Sometimes, she's depicted as a cow or a sow. Other times, she's seen as a bird or a scorpion. This Mother Goddess is a well-known protector. You could say that she was the precursor to the Black Virgin because the images of the Black Virgin we have today were inspired by images of Isis. Both of them are shown with black or dark skin.

There is much-shared symbolism between Isis and the Black Madonna. By looking at either one, you're looking at a picture of them and seeing stories being crafted through the symbols in their art. If you study ancient Egyptian art depicting Isis, you'll notice an ankh in her hand. That symbol isn't just there to look cool. It is the representation of life itself. It is a sign that she's connected to life and rules the process of rebirth. Now, what about the Black Virgin? You can draw a parallel between her and Isis because she is depicted with a child, representing her connection to life and fertility.

Ancient Egyptians believed that Isis was capable of making miracles happen. In their eyes, she was far more than a goddess to be worshiped. You could always turn to her when you needed healing if you were ill. In fact, so powerful was she that she brought the dead back to life. She offered people hope where there was none. Similar to Isis, the Black Virgin also performs miracles. Once more, the millions who flock to Black Madonna sites worldwide annually don't do so for fun and games. They understand the power that this deity holds. They go, hoping that she can miraculously touch their lives. So, when you think about it, you realize that Isis and Black Madonna carry the same essence of the Divine Feminine.

Ceres

This myth is the explanation for the seasons and their cycle, as well as a testament to Ceres's power to transform anything and everyone.

shakko, CC BY-SA 3.0 <https://creativecommons.org/licenses/by-sa/3.0>, via Wikimedia Commons: https://commons.wikimedia.org/wiki/File:Ceres_(Pio-Clementino)_cast_in_Pushkin_museum.jpg

In Roman mythology, you have the goddess Ceres. She is responsible for motherly relationships and fertility. Grain crops and agriculture are also her domain. When she's artistically depicted, you'll see her as a woman of mature years, sitting with a crown of wheat stalks, a sheaf of wheat, torches, and a sickle. You can also find her with cereals and a cornucopia full of fruit. This image clearly depicts fertility and growth, showing that this goddess is a provider, able to nurture one and all. This goddess is held in high esteem because she is connected to the cycles of life and death as well as the seasons. She is considered a nurturer, responsible for introducing mankind to agriculture so that they can nurture themselves. Like Isis, she is also a healer and is connected to growth and fertility.

One of the myths of this goddess features her and her daughter Proserpina, who is Persephone in Greek mythology. Cere's daughter was abducted by Hades, also known as Pluto. By taking her daughter away from her, Pluto caused Ceres deep anguish and pain. Deeply aggrieved,

Ceres decided she was going to fix things. How? She decided not a single crop would grow on the surface of the Earth until she had her daughter back. Things got so dire that Jupiter had to step in and work something out between Ceres and Pluto regarding Proserpina. So, it was agreed that Proserpina would spend a portion of the year with Hades and the other with Ceres. This myth explains the seasons and their cycle, as well as a testament to Ceres's power to transform anything and everyone.

Now, return your attention to the Black Madonna, and you'll notice that both she and Ceres act as nurturers and protectors. They are both capable of miracles and are intercessors who can intercede on your behalf when you need someone to plead your case. Where the Roman goddess transforms the seasons, the Black Madonna does her own transformation on a spiritual level, changing souls for the better.

Cybele

She was the caretaker and nurturer of the Earth itself.
Getty Villa, CC BY-SA 2.0 <https://creativecommons.org/licenses/by-sa/2.0>, via Wikimedia Commons: https://commons.wikimedia.org/wiki/File:Cybele_Getty_Villa_57.AA.19.jpg

This Anatolian goddess is called Mountain Mother. You can trace her origins as far back as the Neolithic times when she was in Çatalhöyük, an Anatolian settlement from 7500 BC to 6400 BC and now an official

UNESCO World Heritage Site. Now, back to Cybele. This Mother Goddess is responsible for fertility. She was the caretaker and nurturer of the Earth itself. In art, you can find her on a throne with lions resting beside her. Sometimes, other wild animals stand in the lions' places. You can't help but get the sense that she is a force to be reckoned with, swift to protect those who come to her and entrust their lives to her.

Like the Black Virgin, Cybele is a nurturer. They are both mother figures, responsible for ensuring life continues as it has always done. In Greece, Cybele's characteristics would be partially assimilated to aspects of Gaia, who rules the Earth. Ancient Romans knew her as Great Mother or Magna Mater, which leaves no doubt that she is a nurturer. One of the myths tells of her lover, Attis, going mad and mutilating himself. When he died, Cybele was beside herself. She did all she could and eventually brought him back to life. In this way, she is depicted as being in charge of life, death, and rebirth.

Both Cybele and the Dark Mother share the traits of nurturing and fertility. You can thank them for the cycles of life, the fertility of the land, or any endeavor you execute successfully. What about creativity? Like the Madonna, Cybele influences that aspect of life as well. You can see it in the way she fosters creative energy. Those who worship her use music, dance, and art in her honor.

Artemis

This goddess reigns supreme over the moon, the wilderness, and the hunt.
Commonists, CC BY-SA 4.0 <https://creativecommons.org/licenses/by-sa/4.0>, via Wikimedia Commons: https://commons.wikimedia.org/wiki/File:Diana_of_Versailles.jpg

Artemis is a goddess worthy of honor and respect. She is the daughter of Leto and Zeus and Apollo's twin. Imagine being transported to Ancient Greece, where you could witness the awe and reverence with which the people honored her. This goddess reigns supreme over the moon, the wilderness, and the hunt. She is usually depicted with hunting knives, a bow, and a quiver full of arrows. Of all the animals and plants there are, she is partial to deer and cypress trees. Undoubtedly, her love for and connection to nature are apparent. For this reason, the Black Madonna has the same love for nature, and some artwork shows her surrounded by lush greenery or other symbols of nature.

By studying Artemis and the Dark Virgin, you'll notice their parallels, archetypally speaking, as they are both nurturers. She's known for taking care of young girls, in particular, keeping them safe. Another interesting parallel is in the aspect of fertility. The Grecian goddess oversees all matters pertaining to midwifery and childbirth, which shows you she's connected to life, fertility, and the cycles that rule one and all.

The Black Madonna and Artemis are known for their association with the moon, the mysteries of the feminine, and wild energy. Sometimes, you'll find the Black Madonna standing confidently on the crescent moon, embodying wildness and the unconscious. Some similarities exist even when it comes to the legends and myths surrounding both of these beings. One of the legends tells of Artemis helping Leto, her mother, so she could birth her twin, Apollo, with ease. Another myth discusses how Artemis kept Leto safe from Hera, Zeus's jealous wife. These stories demonstrate her powerful, benevolent, and protective nature. These traits of Artemis can be found in the Dark Mother, too.

Women turn to Artemis when they need help dealing with the painful experience of childbirth, and she comes through for them. So, like the Dark Virgin, Artemis also performs miracles and swiftly answers sincere prayers. Artemis is also a virgin, like the Dark Madonna. She didn't care for male attention. Her attendants were also expected to remain chaste, and when they broke their chastity vow, they would suffer the consequences. These beings are the epitome of motherhood, godhood, feminine strength, and nature.

Kali

Time, creation, and change are all in her hands, and so are death and destruction, which is why devotees know she's not to be trifled with.

https://commons.wikimedia.org/wiki/File:Kali_lithograph.jpg

Kali is a Hindu goddess who is loved and feared by many, and for good reason. Her power is exceedingly great. Time, creation, and change are all in her hands, and so are death and destruction, which is why devotees know she's not to be trifled with. You see, in Hindu tantric tradition, there are ten Mahavidyas. The word *Mahavidya* means "Great Wisdoms," and they are a group of ten goddesses, including Tara, Tripura Sundari, Bhuvaneshwari, Chhinnamasta, Bhairavi, Baglamukhi, Matangi, Dhumavati, Kamala, and Kali. The first time Kali made herself known to the world was when she manifested from Durga. Her goal was simple: To end all that is evil so that those who are innocent can be free from its terrors. She would come to be known as the Mother of the Universe and the Divine Mother by sects devoted to her.

Interestingly enough, the Black Mother is also called the Queen of the Earth and the Queen of Heaven since she is the transcendent version of the Virgin Mary. On top of that, she represents the Immaculate Conception and incorruptibility. This shows both beings are the same in their opposition to all that is evil and corrupt. The Black Madonna has never given herself over to a man or male deity, nor will she ever.

This Dark Virgin is a protector, similar to Kali, as the latter offers a safe haven for those who trust her. She gives them true liberation.

Mythologically speaking, the Black Madonna and Kali the Destroyer share certain interesting traits. Consider *Sara-la-Kâli*, also known as "Sarah the Black One." Many believe she shares a connection with the Black Mother and will often speak of her in that context. She is honored by gypsies, who see her as their royal ruler, and Catholics. You may wonder what the connection is between Sarala-Kâli and the goddess Kali. Well, this being is the patron saint of the Romani people who originate from India. In case you wondered why she has an English name, in Romani, she is *Sara e Kali*. Sarah or Sara is etymologically Hebrew, meaning "noblewoman" or "princess." Not only that, but you can also find the name *Sara* within the Durga Saptashati, which is an ancient Hindu scripture dedicated to Durga, the Divine Mother herself. In this sacred, ancient text, Durga is called Kali, as well as Sara.

In the Durga Saptashati, you'll find stories of Durga fighting demons who possessed great power, which they used to cause chaos and terrorize the world. The goddess would morph from one form to another to defeat these powerful entities. These stories show how she, like the Dark Mother, fights your battles to protect you from anything and anyone seeking to harm you.

Ala

Ala is a deity of the Igbo tribe in Eastern Nigeria. Her devotees also call her Ali, Ale, Ana, or Ani, depending on the Igbo dialect they speak. Her name literally means "ground," a reference to the extent of her power. Creativity, fertility, morality, and the Earth are her domains, over which she rules gracefully. She also oversees the affairs of the underworld. Like a pregnant woman, she carries the souls of ancestors and the dead in her womb. You can infer that she not only rules the Earth but *is the Earth herself*. She ensures everyone acts justly and fairly, following the rules of the land. Like the Black Madonna, she is known for fertility and is a protector and nurturer. She is also seen as the goddess of love, full of compassion and wisdom.

Ala is depicted as a deity with a regal aura, often with her family around her while she sits on her throne. This is reminiscent of the Black Madonna and her little one, demonstrating motherhood. Her devotees know that when they pray to her, much like the Black Madonna, she answers with a miracle.

Oya

Oya is a Goddess from Western Nigeria. She is also called Yansä in Latin America, where she is known and revered. An orisha, she is in control of violent storms, bringing wind and lightning wherever she sees fit. She's also a river goddess; her devotees see her as overseeing children. Many who have been barren have received the miracle of conception from her as she blessed and continues to bless those who ask with children. Unlike the Black Madonna, she did get married to Sango, the god of thunder. However, they're both known for being nurturing and protective of those they know belong to them. Oya is known for protecting her people from their enemies and any injustice toward them. This is similar to the Black Madonna, who has been known to protect her people from those who sought to oppress them. These deities are also known to cause renewal and radical change as needed. Oya does this through her winds, which can both create and destroy.

In Conclusion

Having read through all the mythologies of these different goddesses across cultures and traditions, it should be obvious that the Black Madonna is the embodiment of the Divine Feminine. From the dawn of time, humanity has been aware of this being or energy. She has gone by multiple names, but now you know her as the Black Madonna. Having read this chapter, it should be difficult to deny the interconnectedness of the Dark Virgin with other mother goddesses from various cultures and times.

Before Christianity, many people had unique beliefs and deities they trusted. These beings shared deep connections with nature and the cycles of life. Among them, you had those with the Mother Goddess archetype. Evidently, beliefs evolve with time. So, when Christianity rose, it strongly influenced how people interacted with spiritual matters. The Christian missionaries did all they could to spread their way of interacting with the divine far and wide. Sometimes, that meant looking for parallels between Christian tenets and the elements that made up the traditional religious beliefs of the people they hoped to convert. It was much easier to convince people to become Christians by helping them see how their present beliefs paralleled the Christian faith. Some say this is how the earth goddesses of old would eventually become the Black Madonna. Regardless of what happened, the fact remains she serves as a bridge to connect all beliefs. Within her dark skin, you can find the unification of all spiritual truths. This esoteric theory should make it clear how and why the Black Madonna has so many similarities with the ancient Mother Goddesses that you have learned about. In the next chapter, you will learn more esoteric interpretations of this mysterious being.

Chapter 6: Esoteric Interpretations

The Black Madonna is associated with divine mysteries and esoteric aspects of spirituality. In this chapter, you will learn about this deity's esoteric and mystical interpretations. As you already know, she is full of symbolism. The question is, what do these symbols mean? How can you make them more personal to you? The way to reap the rewards of her symbolism is through understanding them. Therefore, The first step will be to explain what esotericism is and why it is important when studying spirituality.

Understand Esotericism

Esotericism is about diving into knowledge to discover deeper meaning, which is often hidden and difficult to spot at first glance. There are certain practices and beliefs which only a few people understand on a deep level. You may be looking at a religious text or considering a particular deity and not immediately notice the deeper layers of meaning to them. Why? These esoteric aspects of a belief or religion are meant to take time to grasp. They require deep contemplation and reflection.

The word "esoteric" is etymologically rooted in esôterikos, a Greek word that means "within" or "inner." This is not your average kind of knowledge. For the most part, people only have knowledge that is publicly available or exoteric. However, when you know something esoterically, it means you have come to discover the truth of that thing from within yourself. When you think of the esoteric, you can think of things like the occult, mysticism, and spirituality. All of these things serve to help you have a better understanding of how life works and your place in it.

Several principles govern esotericism. Before considering the esoteric nature of the Black Madonna, you should understand what these principles are about.

The Principle of Hidden Knowledge: Esoteric knowledge is never publicly available. Usually, this information is shared between the master, who has come to understand the spiritual subjects, and the students, who seek to learn. So, people will journey to ashrams, shrines, or other sacred places, hoping to receive esoteric knowledge from those in the know. Esoteric knowledge requires secrecy. Not everyone gets to understand it. This is because only some are prepared to handle the power that comes with esoteric knowledge. Some people may not know what to do with it, while others may use the knowledge for nefarious intentions. This is why esoteric knowledge is only given to a select few. A second reason for this selectivity is to prevent the message from being diluted or corrupted in some way. All esoteric knowledge is profound and sacred. When you truly understand how the universe works, it makes you a powerful person. What you do with that power is another matter entirely. This is why the keepers of esoteric knowledge jealously guard what they know. These people have the responsibility of safeguarding wisdom that is timeless and ancient.

The Principle of Spiritual Evolution: The evolution of the human spirit is another principle behind esoteric knowledge. Everyone has the ability to experience personal growth and achieve true transformation from within, which then leads to them being enlightened. You are no exception. The truly esoteric person understands that it is possible to develop spiritually – but also *necessary.* Only when you consciously develop your spiritual journey can you experience deeper self-awareness and access states of consciousness higher than you are accustomed to.

The truly esoteric person understands that it is not only possible to develop spiritually but also necessary.
https://pixabay.com/illustrations/meditation-spiritual-yoga-1384758/

Your soul is on a journey. As it goes down its path, it must evolve. When you understand the esoteric and live your life according to its principles, you will go beyond regular everyday experiences. Things that used to bother you deeply will no longer be a problem because you can see past what your reality is showing you.

The first step to becoming spiritually developed is realizing you have an ego. The ego consists of all the stories you've told yourself. It is everything you believe to be true about yourself. The moment you realize you are far more than your ego, you evolve past these limiting stories and beliefs you have. You see how your ego is not your true self but a tool to be used by your soul to experience life. Therefore, to practice esotericism, you need to be willing to self-reflect to become more aware of your authentic nature. You'd be hard-pressed to find a better way to do this than through mindfulness and meditation on the Black Madonna and her essence.

The Principle of Symbolism and Allegory: Every esoteric tradition understands and accepts that symbolism and allegory are important. Words can only do so much to transmit meaning so that you can truly understand the topic. However, symbolism is an excellent way to get the meaning of an idea deep into your soul. The same can be said for allegories. As a human being, you naturally tend to pay attention to stories. You could argue your everyday existence is full of stories. Every person is a walking book full of stories, too. The classic three-act structure is one that humans resonate with because everyone is wired to understand stories. So, what better ways would there be to encapsulate the deeper meanings of esoteric concepts than through stories?

Understand that symbols are far more than simple representations of ideas. Think of each one as a doorway or a portal that allows you access to a deeper and even more real version of reality than you've ever known. Symbols and allegories cut through the mundane and ordinary, allowing you to reach deep into the heart of the archetypes that make up life. In esotericism, each symbol carries far more meaning than you can glean when you are first introduced to it. Through regular contemplation and meditation upon the symbol, you find yourself peeling back the layers to discover even richer meanings. Think of it like a tree trunk with concentric circles, except in esotericism, the circles never end.

The Principle of Divine Connection: Esotericism implies that you are connected to divinity. Unlike other traditional religious systems, Esotericism shows you do not need an intermediary to access spiritual powers or enlightenment. You have the power to transform yourself, and you can do so without any help. Traditional religion insists that you must go through some intermediary. In those rigid structures, there is a need for hierarchy. This can be rather limiting to the psyche and soul. Therefore, esotericism is a liberator. It helps you break the traditional religious chains that hold you back and allows you direct access to the divine source that created you.

The beautiful thing about being an esotericist is you know you can contact the source or creator of all things. You know you aren't limited by your background or what you believe in terms of religion. You know the divine does not care where you stand in society. You deeply understand that your connection to divinity supersedes every possible limitation that people can come up with. Sure, you may belong to a certain religious group. You may take part in certain religious activities. However, you are also aware of the freedom you have to get in touch with the source of life directly.

The Principle of Holistic Understanding: As an esotericist, you realize that life can be understood on a holistic level. It is tough to deny the interconnectedness of concepts, ideas, and all created things. The more aware you become of yourself and how the universe works by diving deeper into esoteric knowledge, the more you will notice the profound connections between seemingly unrelated things. This is the principle of holistic understanding, where you can learn the truth about life, from how a butterfly flies to how marketers entice people to purchase a product.

The true esotericist understands that there are connections between the physical and spiritual world, even if they may not be immediately apparent. They know the created world is simply the microcosm of the macrocosm. Look around you. If you pay close attention and truly ponder it, you will notice that everything around you is a reflection of a deeper spiritual force or principle. Whether you look at life through the lens of mysticism, astrology, alchemy, or anything else, you will notice it's all interwoven. Every field of study is part of the puzzle that makes up existence. As an esotericist, it is your job to find the thread that connects all these things and to use what you learn from the connections to develop your soul. You learn the importance of seeing beyond the superficial. You never make the mistake of assuming that something is irrelevant. As a result, you can find patterns in everything. Perceiving and understanding the patterns is key to developing your life spiritually and in every other aspect.

The Esoteric Origins of the Black Madonna

Now that you understand the fundamental principles of esotericism, it is time to discover why it should be a key part of approaching your relationship with the Black Madonna. However, before getting into that, here is a close look at the esoteric origins of the Black Madonna.

The Unification of All Ancient Earth Goddesses: In a previous chapter, you discovered how the Black Madonna shares ties with ancient Earth goddesses. Humanity has always been aware of the Divine Feminine, so the feminine deity has always been worshiped. Since the dawn of time, humanity has been aware of the energy that drives the cycles of life. People are drawn by the desire to honor this energy, which is responsible for the abundance and fertility that everyone enjoys. People from prehistoric times would worship an Earth goddess representing this feminine force. They understood that when it came to being nurtured and protected, they owed their thanks to this force.

So, the Black Madonna, with her dark skin, represents this archetype from ancient times. Her dark skin is reminiscent of the Earth, with its rich, fertile soil, which is responsible for allowing food to grow and sustaining all of life. So, esoterically speaking, the Black Madonna is a connection between the sacredness of Mother Earth and all the mysteries surrounding the creation process.

The Mystery of Alchemy: Next, there's the matter of the connection between the Black Madonna and alchemy, a process that involves turning base metals into gold. Some say this process is only figurative, while others believe there are actual alchemists who successfully transformed base metals into gold. Either way, the transformation process happens within you. Somewhere along the line, there is a point where you no longer exist the way you've always known yourself. Some people call this ego death, while in alchemy, it is known as the *nigredo*. This is a stage of darkness. Everything you thought you knew about who you are is suddenly dissolved. This is another esoteric interpretation of the dark skin of the Madonna. However, from the darkness emerges the gold you carry within you. What is this gold in the spiritual context? It is your enlightenment.

The Mystery Schools and Their Initiation Rites: Remember, one of the tenets of esotericism is the fact that it is selective and secret. For the longest time, there have been different mystery schools that only allow those who qualify for initiation access to the knowledge they carry. The Black Madonna herself is an enigma. Her mystery finds its roots in the ancient traditions. Those who attended ancient mystery schools to learn more about her realized she embodies inner transformation. They knew she alone carries true spiritual insights that radically transform and empower you. They did not share this information with the masses but kept it for those who truly seek deep experiences with the Black Madonna. Think of her esoterically as the portal to spiritual insight and truth. She makes it so you don't have to find an ancient mystery school. Instead, you can come to her with an open heart and seek the light of her wisdom.

Hermetic and Gnostic Touches: Hermetic and Gnostic traditions are well known for encouraging you to experience inner illumination and deepen your spiritual practice. With deep study, you will notice the connection between the Black Madonna and Hermetic and Gnostic values. For one thing, the color black is not seen as a devilish or evil thing. It is understood under these principles that there is so much more to black than darkness and negativity. Instead, in Hermeticism and Gnosticism, black is seen as the material from which all of life emerges. It is understood that all spiritual insight comes from darkness.

The Alchemy of the Soul

The first stage of soul alchemy involves the blackening, where everything dissolves into utter chaos. Your consciousness feels like it has descended into darkness. This is *nigredo*, where you finally face the shadow self you've been avoiding your whole life. You realize there is no way out than to go through the challenge you are dealing with. The blackness of the Dark Virgin is representative of this stage of alchemy. She represents what it means to go through the dark night of the soul.

Next comes the albedo. When experiencing this stage of alchemy, it feels as if someone cracked a window and let some light in. You feel as if you are being purified. Little by little, you gain more clarity about what you should do in life and feel enlightened. The Black Madonna symbolizes the duality of life. She carries within her both darkness and light. So, this stage of the alchemy of your soul represents the light essence of the Madonna.

Finally, you experience the *rubedo*. This final alchemical stage refers to the transformation of your soul. At this point, you realize that you were never separate from divinity. You only perceived yourself to be that way. When you get to this stage of transformation, you find yourself expressing the transcendent nature of the Black Madonna. You experience what it means to be connected to heaven and earth. This is the point where you finally realize that there is no way anyone could separate you from the love of the Creator.

There is an extra element to the alchemical transformation of your soul. It is the realization that you will always carry within you both your light and dark aspects. Some assume enlightenment means they will never relapse into a place of darkness. However, there will always be new levels of enlightenment to attain. Each time, you will experience something akin to the darkness of the soul. When you accept this, your dark knights are far easier to handle. You no longer allow yourself to wallow as you did in the past, and in fact, you become excited because you know your breakthrough will be beyond anything you've ever imagined possible for yourself.

It is terrible to experience the dark night of the soul, thinking there is no one to support you. However, when you become aware of the Black Madonna and this period hits you, it's comforting to know she has your back. She is a steadfast and true friend, a companion who will never abandon you, no matter how ugly things may seem. This is what you are experiencing right now. Dare to surrender yourself to her. Dare to trust that she will help you find the enlightenment you need to pull yourself out of the hole you are in. Dare to trust that the darkness is not permanent, and eventually, the sun will rise in your life again.

The Cosmic Cycle

Esoterically, the Black Madonna is a dance of rhythms. You find up and down within her, high and low, ebb and flow. One of the rhythms in this being is darkness and creation. The Madonna represents the primordial darkness from which everything created in the world comes. When you think about darkness, what comes to your mind? Do you assume it is the absence of light? This is not the sort of darkness being referred to here in the context of the Black Madonna's esoteric interpretation.

The African Mother's darkness is a powerful and creative one. It is the womb of all things and beings in existence and to exist. It is the same womb where you can expect your soul to be transformed for good. This black color, which the Black Madonna carries, represents the cosmic void unrestricted by time. This same void births and carries the galaxies and stars you see. The darkness draws you, asking you to plunge into the depths of your spiritual aspects and see what gold you can emerge with.

There is also a dance between the Divine Feminine and the Divine Masculine. As already explained, the Black Madonna epitomizes the feminine principle. However, there is a need for balance in your spiritual life, which is why the Divine Masculine is a necessary counterpart. At first glance, it may not seem like it, but the Black Madonna has symbolism that shows the essential nature of the Divine Masculine. You see, she has a strong connection to the Earth and is connected to light and darkness. Since she represents cycles and rhythms, it only makes sense that she also carries within her the Divine Masculine, an active force that is necessary for transformation. To sum it all up, the Black Madonna is responsible for integrating opposites. This is a reminder that you must discover the dual natures within yourself and accept them as valid.

The Rewards of the Exploring the Black Madonna's Esotericism

You Will Realize the Depth of Symbolism When you approach your study and understanding of the Black Madonna with esotericism. You will discover a symbolic depth to this deity. Think about her dark skin, for instance. What else could you glean from the information you have received from this book about what her skin represents? If you want more information on the symbolism of her dark skin, it would be best for you to meditate on it. When you spend time deeply contemplating the Black Madonna's dark skin, you will receive levels of knowledge and insight that others may not have. What's the best part? The information you receive will be unique to you and your life experience. So, it would be in your best interest to begin thinking of the Black Madonna from an esoteric point of view. If you ever feel stuck when trying to understand a certain aspect of this being, you can ask her for help. She will gladly help you discover useful insights.

You Will Discover New Depths of Connection to Her. You use esoteric practices like prayer and meditation to connect with the Black Madonna. You will discover the depth of the connection you share with the divine. Like it or not, you are always connected to your source. You only think you are not because you have not allowed yourself to see it. So, an interesting thing starts to happen when you meditate upon the Black Madonna's image or essence, pray to her, or contemplate what she means to you. You approach everything from the mundane to the most important, from a spiritual place. With constant esoteric practices to connect you to the Black Madonna, you receive deep spiritual insights that you've never had before. These insights will open up within you and give you a profound understanding you could never receive from any book or guru out there. Books, videos, gurus, teachers, and whatever else in the exterior world can only teach you so much. However, you will achieve true transformation when you decide you desire esoteric knowledge concerning the Black Madonna.

You Will be Reborn and Transformed into a More Transcendent Version of Yourself. Once more, the Black Madonna is known for her power over rebirth and transformation. You already know the core tenets of esotericism, which include personal development and spiritual growth. When you work with the Black Madonna and seek esoteric knowledge, you will undoubtedly become different. As she gives you new insight, you will begin to think, speak, and act through that filter. For instance, if you are a workaholic, and the Dark Virgin reveals the essence of rest and allowing things to manifest on their own, you may begin to take things easy and seek more time to relax. With your new appreciation for rest and relaxation, you may notice even how you walk is different. You take deeper breaths. You stop trying to rush things. You understand that everything happens in its own time. As a result, the people who have always known you may find that you are a completely different person. You also will attest to the fact that you feel different now. You start prioritizing ease and flow over struggle and strife. You wonder how it is that you could have ever lived any other way. You realize that resting and choosing ease and flow allows even greater abundance in life and more progress regarding your career. Eventually, it occurs to you that your old self is dead. You have experienced true transformation. You are reborn.

Chapter 7: Connecting with the Black Madonna

You're still reading this book, which further affirms that you really are drawn to the Black Madonna. She beckons you, asking you to give life with her a try. However, before you commit fully and take the plunge, it's worth asking yourself what you hope to experience by having her in your life. What motive do you have for wanting to connect with the Divine Mother? If you can answer this question clearly and sincerely, you're going to experience what you seek and then some.

Answering the Virgin's Call: Growing Inner Resonance

So, you want to understand why you're connecting with the Black Virgin, which means you need time and space to reflect. You must be intentional about it whenever you are ready to do this. Pick a time you'll use for this exercise. The room you're in should be quiet and comfortable. Adjust the lighting so it's ambient rather than harsh. If you can't find some quiet because of others around you, you may want to do this exercise when everyone else is asleep. Alternatively, you could use a white noise machine or play white noise on the internet using your headphones or speakers to drown out the noise around you. You're about to get in touch with yourself, so you want it to be just you with your thoughts, no distractions, no interruptions.

So, you want to understand why you're connecting with the Black Virgin, which means you need time and space to reflect.
https://pixabay.com/illustrations/aware-awake-accepting-attuned-1353780/

Openness: You have to start with an open mind. Have no expectations about how or when the Black Virgin will answer you. *Trust that she will.* Trust that when she answers, whether during this exercise or some other day, you'll know it without a doubt. Now, shut your eyes and breathe deeply. Allow your heart to be open. You're doing this with a curious, exploring mind that seeks to learn, not one that's convinced it knows all there is to know. If you start with this attitude, you'll surely discover what your motives are.

Reflection: Now, it's time to reflect on what about the Black Virgin draws you to her. Do you love the fact that she's an enigma? Perhaps you know she has so many secrets and profound insights to share with you, and you're excited to put them into practice in your life. Is there a certain esoteric truth about her that calls you? Do you love that she so effortlessly embodies light and darkness without elevating one over the other? Could it be that you enjoy the thought of the peace she offers your heart, mind, and soul? Are you seeking release from pain and suffering that has become difficult to bear? The only way to know what you seek is to ask yourself questions like these. You could consider the aspects of your life you feel dissatisfied with. If you're unhappy with every part of your life, that's okay too. There's nothing too big or too small for the Black Madonna to help you with. Be candid with yourself as you ask these questions. You may speak with yourself aloud or in your mind. For best results, you should use a journal because you'll have something to refer to later on, and you'll be glad to note how your motives to connect with the Mother evolve.

Emotions: During this self-reflection exercise, you may notice interesting emotions bubbling to the surface. You could feel anything from restless longing to comfort as you think about her. Trust that whatever emotion bubbles up is supposed to be there. If you ask yourself, "Why do I feel this way right now?" and sit with the question, you will discover interesting insights. The answers will clue you in on why you want to connect with the Black Virgin. Let them flow onto the page of your journal, holding nothing back. The Black Virgin does not judge you for your feelings or thoughts, so you don't have to worry about putting on a show of holiness and piety. Write your feelings, raw and unfiltered. Let it all flow.

The Past: It's time to dive into your past. This portion of the exercise isn't meant to make you feel regret, shame, pain, or judge yourself negatively. You're combing through your past for experiences that resonate with the Black Virgin's essence and symbolism. You're looking for times when she may have shown up for you, but you weren't aware it was her. Recall the darkest, lowest points in your life. You know them. Those were times when you were desperate for guidance, longing for a healing touch, thirsty for change but unsure how to make it happen. Look for signs the Black Virgin was with you, and if you can't think of any, turn your attention to how she could have been a great comfort and help if you knew you could call upon her and receive miracles.

Release: Digging through your past is uncomfortable. You may find yourself caught in the throes of the negativity, anger, hurt, shame, and heaviness that gripped you. This is a good thing. It's an opportunity for you to release those emotions. Do not judge them or the experiences that led to them as terrible. Instead, welcome the feelings that flood your mind and body. Sit with them, and allow them to lead you. You may find your writing gets more frantic and erratic. Perhaps you have the urge to scream or cry. Do that. Don't bottle anything in. What you're doing right now is choosing to accept every aspect of yourself, and that includes the part of you that suffered and probably is still in pain.

Clarity: Now, turn your attention to what you'd like to experience by becoming one with the African Mother and making her a real presence in your life. You'll have some answers come to mind at this point. Write them down, then continue to drill past the surface by asking why. "Why do I want that?" When you get an answer, ask the question again. Continue until you drill down to the core of what your soul hungers for. When you know how you'd like the Black Mother to feed you, allowing her to satisfy you becomes easier when you officially welcome her into your life.

A Deeper Connection: Inner Resonance and Intuition

You may know many people who profess a certain faith, but for whatever reason, you can tell their connection to it isn't strong. They don't take it seriously. They're religious or spiritual on paper, and that's about it. Well, you're going to avoid making the same mistake they do. If you want to make this work, you must be in touch with your intuition. Everyone has intuition. If you split the words, you get "in" and "tuition." This is teaching, wisdom, and guidance that comes from within you. The odds are you're an intuitive person, seeing as you've been drawn to this book. However, if you get the sense that you could develop your intuition further, you should. You see, you need that inner guidance to help you understand your true self and your motives for desiring the Mother's healing heart and loving light in your life.

So, what is inner resonance? How does that help you connect with the Black Mother on a deep level? Think about your favorite song. If you can, listen to it right now. As it plays, notice the way you feel. If it's a happy song, you feel your mood lift. If it's a sad song, you feel your mood shift to reflect that sadness, or if you were already sad before listening, you will feel your sadness deepen. That's how inner resonance works. It is what you experience when you feel something on a level so deep, it's soul-deep. So, when you initiate contact with the Black Virgin, you'll notice the same thing. It's like there's a force tugging on your soul. You may not have the words to describe your experience, but it will feel like you know her. It will appear you've become one with her, and you "get" her. Her thoughts and emotions become yours. You find unity between your mind and the symbolism of the Mother. This is pure resonance.

Now, return to the matter of your intuition. Your intuition will confirm that the resonance you feel is real. It lets you know you are in the presence of the Divine Feminine herself. Your intuition could be a gentle voice on the inside. It could feel like a strong knowing. It will often show up using the language of feelings. The further you go on your journey with the Black Virgin, the stronger your intuition will become, and the deeper your connection with her will be. So, listen to your inner voice. It knows where you should go. If you allow it, you'll feel guided. It's like an invisible hand on your shoulder; its touch is gentle as it steers you down the right path. It could feel like an urge to learn even more than you have about the Dark Mother. It could be a desire to shut your doors, shut your eyes, and sit quietly contemplating her grace and love. Whatever it is you're feeling, trust it. Intuition is your soul speaking to you through the language of your feelings.

Developing Stronger Intuition

You now understand intuition is important, and it would only serve you to get better at using it. So, what practical ways can you strengthen your intuitive muscles?

Try Meditation. How? Meditation is a mindfulness practice where you focus on one thing for some time and nothing else. Typically, meditators focus on their breath or some other steady sound. You could do this or get a picture or some other visual representation of the Black Virgin and keep your attention on her. When your mind wanders away from whatever you have chosen to focus on, gently return your attention where it belongs. Beating yourself up about losing focus is a waste of time and will set you back. Meditation is mastering your attention and awareness, and the fact that you keep noticing you've been distracted is good for you. With time and practice, you'll find the moments of distraction decrease. People who have meditated for years even develop the ability to meditate in the chaos of busy traffic. However, you need time to get to this point. You will only enjoy the benefits of meditation if you practice every day. So, set aside five to ten minutes when you can sit in silence to meditate. With time, you can increase the duration of your sessions.

Journal Daily. When you journal, you're getting in touch with yourself. You're checking in, seeking where you're at relative to where you've been. You're engaged in a dialogue with yourself, using the medium of paper. Your journal should contain the events of the day, how you feel about them, how you feel about yourself, your spiritual journey, insights you receive from within, intuitive messages, dreams, patterns you've noticed, and anything else that comes to mind. By journaling, you strengthen the connection between your mind and soul, making it easier to pick up on intuitive messages and tell them apart from random thoughts.

Spend Time in Nature. Nature is an excellent tool to help you become a more intuitive person. You could be up in the mountains, deep in the heart of the forest, or by a babbling brook. It doesn't matter, as long as you're surrounded by nature. When you're in natural settings, it does wonders for your intuition. You're removed from the daily stresses and chaos that demand your attention. Instead, you're in Mother Nature's presence. You're sitting with the Black Virgin herself. The more time you spend in her energy in nature, the better you'll be at hearing her call and responding.

Nature is an excellent tool to help you become a more intuitive person.
https://www.pexels.com/photo/woman-spreading-both-her-arms-2529375/

Pay Attention to Your Dreams. There's no better medium for your soul or the spirit world to reach you than through your dreams. So, keep a dream journal. When you wake, don't be in a hurry to open your eyes and roll out of bed. Don't move. Remain where you are, and allow the last image from your dream to come to you. Then, you can work your way backward. When you've remembered it all, you can then journal. If you get up too fast, move around too much, or allow your mind to begin its habitual worrying and planning for the day, you may forget your dreams.

If you are one of those people who can't recall their dreams, or you think you don't dream, what do you do? Remain in bed, eyes shut, body still and relaxed, and pay attention to how you feel. Sit with the feeling, and then write that in your journal. Don't be surprised when you start remembering your dreams. The more you journal them, the easier it will be to recall them because you've taught your subconscious mind that it is important to remember your dreams. So, it will facilitate your dream recall.

Notice What Your Body Is Doing. Sometimes, you'll get an intuitive feeling so strong you feel it in your body. Your body has wisdom. It is wiser than you realize. So, whenever you need to make a decision, notice the way you feel. Is there some tightness or heaviness in your chest? That could tell you there's something wrong with the option you've selected. Do you feel light in your chest? Is your breathing deep and sure? The odds are you've chosen the best path for you at this time, so you should proceed with your decision and trust it. Some people get an instant headache or tummy ache when they meet people who are no good. Is this you? Recall instances when you had to make a critical decision. Think back to when you first met someone who wound up being toxic. Remember when you met the people you feel most at home with? Can you recall how those experiences went? Can you reenact them in your mind and pay attention to the feeling you get in your body? This is how to master your body's intuitive signals.

Decide to Trust Your Intuition. Some people receive intuitive messages, but they dismiss them as nothing-burgers. They don't act on what they get. When you ignore the messages from within, you weaken your ability to perceive them. The same thing happens when you doubt what you're being told. So, decide to trust your gut, regardless of how it plays out. Whenever you get a strong feeling or are nudged to do something, follow through with no questions asked and no expectations. You will be tempted to "logic" your way out of acting. However, you must accept that logic is severely limited when it comes to matters of the spirit. You cannot attempt to contain the unspeakable, unimaginable vastness of spirit in the small, rigid cage of logic. Otherwise, you'll not only be unable to sense when your intuition is telling you something, but you'll also live a needlessly difficult life.

Whichever route you choose to help you develop your intuition, you should be patient with yourself. This development will take time. Suppose you attempt to rush the process or get upset with yourself for not seeing results sooner. In that case, you'll only slow your progress or stop it altogether.

A Guided Meditation Practice

Guided meditation is similar to meditation, except your attention will be on what your guide says. You'll be asked to visualize or feel things. If you worry you can't visualize, understand it's no different than imagining something in your mind. Some people can use all their senses in their imagination with no problem, while others may be better at feeling, hearing, or something else. Whatever the case is for you, you can still work with this guided meditation by imagining it is true, even if your inner visuals or other senses aren't that clear.

Starting Out: You need to be somewhere peaceful. If other people are around you, ask them to leave you alone for the next ten to fifteen minutes. Turn off all your devices, as you want to avoid being dragged out of this meditation by an inconvenient notification. Wear comfortable clothing that doesn't itch or feel too tight, and sit or lie comfortably. Place your feet flat on the floor if you're sitting on a chair. Your back should be straight, but not uncomfortably so. Picture a wire that's connected to the top of your head. Imagine someone pulling it, causing you to straighten your posture. If you're sitting on the floor, you may sit in an easy lotus position. You could also sit with your feet stretched out in front or in any other position that will allow you to relax. Shut your eyes and begin breathing deeply. As you breathe, allow your mind to quieten and let your body relax. Remember your intention; you want to invite the Black Madonna into your space and your life.

Visualizing: Picture yourself in a forest. The greens are vibrant, the sounds are pleasant, and the aura of that space is one of tranquility. You love being here. You enjoy watching the warm, golden sun dancing on the floor as it comes through the leaves being rustled by the wind, which feels delicious on your skin. You feel drawn to look up ahead of you and give in to the urge. As you do, you sense the Black Madonna's presence. She's not far now. She can't be. She's the reason this sacred space exists.

You walk further down the forest path, which is strewn with brown leaves on either side. Some of those leaves are on the path, too. They crinkle and crunch beneath your feet, adding to the sense of serenity and sacredness of the forest. You come to a stop when you see a female figure before you. Her form is adorned with a robe that flows elegantly. Her face is the picture of peace and serenity. You look in her eyes, twin dark orbs full of ancient wisdom and the knowledge of things too wondrous to capture with words. You notice her skin is dark. It's like it whispers to you that it carries the deepest of mysteries. It tells you it nurtures the cosmos and can nurture you, too. This being is the Black Madonna.

Making the Connection: Now, allow yourself to feel her energy. Let it flood you, body and soul. Notice how it feels warm. It reminds you of being swaddled in soft, comforting blankets as a child. You feel her around you, embracing you gently. Her love permeates you, and you feel it in your chest. You notice your heart welling up with love for her, and you can tell she is also filling you with her love for you. As you remain in her embrace, you feel at one with her. You feel a connection, one you've never had with anyone before. It's a deep connection that feels like the ground is no longer beneath your feet. Instead, you're deep in the heart of the ocean of the Dark Mother's love. Each breath makes your body thrill with joy and ecstasy. You wish you could deepen this feeling, this love you sense from her embrace. In response, you feel her presence and comfort even more intensely since she knows your desires even before you ask. You notice tears spring to your eyes, and you're fine with that. You feel you've known her for many lifetimes, and the truth is, you have.

Conversing: The connection is now complete. You and the Black Madonna are now bonded. She is part of your life and willing to listen to you. So, speak with her. You could speak aloud, in your mind, or under your breath. Do whatever feels natural to you. Let her know whatever is in your heart. You could ask her your questions, tell her what you desire, or just let her know you're only here to enjoy her presence and spend time with her. You could ask her for wisdom and guidance regarding a specific matter, healing, or anything else. If you don't know what to ask for, you could just keep thanking her in anticipation of the wonders she will perform in your life.

Listening: It's now time to sit in the silence. Sit in expectation, and the Black Virgin will respond. She may use actual words or communicate with you through feelings. She may conjure up symbols, and their meaning will become apparent to you right then or at a later time. She may simply flood your heart with her peace and love. This is how she offers guidance to you and affirms she has heard and handled your concerns.

Becoming One with the Mother: Now, feel your own energy. Then, shift your focus to the Black Virgin's energy. Move your attention back and forth from your energy to hers, sitting with each one for a moment. Finally, allow your energy and hers to merge. Notice how it creates something new. Notice the intuitive knowing that you're now a different person, that you have been blessed spiritually, and that blessing will play out in other aspects of your life. By merging your energies, you solidify and strengthen your bond with the Mother.

Show Gratitude: When you feel it's time, thank the Black Madonna for showing up for you. Thank her for guiding you and loving you unconditionally. Thank her because you know just because this meditation is coming to a close doesn't mean she will be far from you. On the contrary, she is now as close to you as you are to your beating heart. Feel her love flowing through your body and mind as you express your love and gratitude to her.

Wrapping Up: As slowly as possible, return your attention to your physical space by first becoming aware of your breath. Then, focus on your body and notice how you feel in it. After a few more breaths, you may open your eyes. Take a few more deep breaths, and then you're done. You have now officially accepted the Black Madonna's invitation. You now carry her presence with you, all day, every day, everywhere. You can continue strengthening the bond between you by using this guided meditation each day.

When you return to your responsibilities and plans for the day, remember you always carry her with you. Even in situations in which you can't take a moment to meditate, know you can communicate with her in your mind. You can always reach out to her at any moment you desire. What happens if you don't meditate and connect with her each day? While she'll remain with you, you may find it more difficult to notice her presence in your life. So, the onus is on you to maintain your connection to her. As for the Black Virgin, she has no intention of letting you go. You'll never have to feel alone again.

Chapter 8: Healing through the Divine Feminine

Divine Healing

When you experience divine healing, you know it. It's unmistakable. You feel it in your body. You notice it in the way your mind works differently. You see the way your life changes for the better. It's like a soothing balm has been spread over your heart, and all your broken bits are whole once again. Whenever you're struggling physically, spiritually, emotionally, or any other way, healing is what you need to restore you to balance.

The Divine Feminine is the force that bandages you up and makes you as good as new. It does more than heal the wounds you're conscious about. It also heals the pain you didn't realize you still have, and that's the beauty of it. Or, put more accurately, that's the beauty of the Dark Mother's healing presence in your life. You know how children always turn to their mothers whenever they're hurt, ill, or wounded? Well, you are the Black Madonna's child. You can turn to her. You're never too old or too sophisticated to take all your pain to her and ask her to show you compassion and healing. She wants you to come to her first whenever you're broken and hurt so she can fix you up and comfort you.

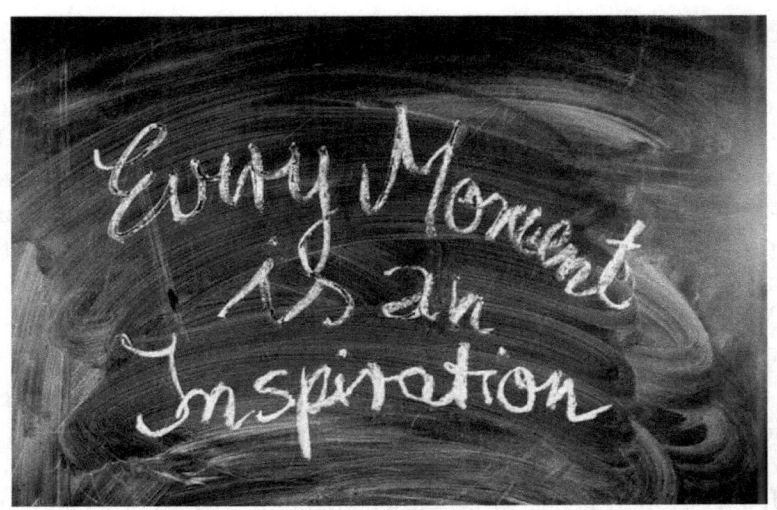

You see, choosing to allow her into your life means you will shed everything blocking your enlightenment.
https://pixabay.com/illustrations/board-writing-chalk-blackboard-953151/

What makes divine healing special is that it goes beyond dressing your emotional and spiritual wounds. The Dark Virgin does far more than fix what's broken in your life. She transforms you from the inside out. She takes your wounds and uses them to ignite the process of rebirth in your heart, giving you a new lease on life. She's not one to let you wallow in pain to get you to learn some lesson. She teaches as she heals you, making her the perfect mother. With time, you'll find she's done more than restore you to your previous state; she has helped you transcend the person you were. You'll find you've become more than the restrictive stories you used to tell and believe about yourself.

The Mother's divine healing is expressed with love, compassion, and empathy. It doesn't get any better than that. Even if you're in a place in life where you feel complete, by inviting her to be with you, you'll be surprised to find there are things that she can transform. You see, choosing to allow her into your life means you will shed everything blocking your enlightenment. Your old wounds may resurface so they can be healed fully. You'll let go of the self-doubt, pain, anger, and fear you've repressed because that was the only way to survive.

The Dark Mother is always there to help you see you're not alone. She is with you at all times. She is there to comfort you, listen to you without judgment, and help you recover from whatever has broken your spirit. She welcomes your vulnerability and accepts you as you are. Let her work her miracles in your life; you'll find every imbalance corrected. If you pay attention, you'll notice most people don't live a life of balance. They either work too much or not at all. They are in a hurry or locked to the couch. They're anxious or apathetic. If you have ever heard someone echo the sentiment, "I'm either here or there. I do extremes, no in-betweens," this is what it means to live a life without balance. Perhaps you, too, have said this once in your life or agree with the sentiment. However, that doesn't have to be the case. Remember, the Dark Virgin epitomizes balance and the integration of opposites. So, you can expect her to teach you to find peace by being balanced.

As the African Virgin heals you, you'll become a pro at aligning your energies. You'll learn how to balance your emotions. For instance, some people genuinely don't understand how to be angry with someone they love. It's as though it has to be either anger or love. They can't fathom how to balance that. So, because they want to be good partners, they'll repress their feelings whenever their partner does something that makes them angry. By the time they let their anger out, they forget this person they're skinning alive is someone they love. When harsh words have been spoken, and hurtful irreversible things have been said, they feel regret, wishing they had reined themselves in. This is just one way the Virgin teaches you how to balance your feelings and every other aspect of life. So, you see, the divine healing from the Black Madonna's love is second to none and beyond compare.

Sophie's Healing

Sophie calls southern France her home, having lived there all her life. Ask anyone who knew her, and they would describe her as a kind, gentle, loving soul, a woman with deep, unwavering faith. Her faith was something to be admired because, for over ten years, she struggled with a debilitating condition. Each day was full of fatigue and pain. She had lived with pain for so long that she didn't remember what it felt like to not have her body aching and feeling like it was falling apart. She always believed that one day, she would find her healing. However, she didn't know how. Her medication only did so much, and some days, she almost lost her faith. Still, she persevered.

One day, a friend swung by Sophie's place with several books for her as she loved to read. Once alone, she picked up the stack of books to see which one she'd get into first. However, the one on the Black

Madonna fell on the floor. It fell awkwardly, open and face down on the ground. Carefully, she reached down to pick it up. Her gut said to read the page that it had fallen open on. So, she did. It turned out that page was about how the Black Madonna heals anyone who asks for her help. At that moment, it felt as though a light went on in her heart. She knew in her heart she had been waiting for this moment.

Sophie would excitedly ring her friend the next day and ask to be taken to the closest Black Madonna shrine. It wasn't an easy journey for Sophie since her body was battered and hurting. Still, with a smile on her lips and a heart full of hope and positive expectation, she made it. When she got to the shrine, she gasped at the statue of the Black Madonna. It was breathtaking to her. It seemed to beckon her closer, and it moved her so deeply she moved closer to it, tears streaming down her face and prayer springing from her lips. She allowed herself to share her pain with the Black Virgin. She cried, "I've had to carry this pain for far too long. Please. I know you are the one I have been waiting for. I know I was meant to be here now. I know you can help me, Black Madonna. I offer you my body, and I ask you to heal me." She reached out to touch the Black Madonna, and while her body still hurt, she felt profound peace in that instant. It was undeniable. Sophie knew the Black Madonna was real and present.

As the days and weeks passed, Sophie experienced a change in her body. She became more flexible. The aches and pains were fewer and fewer. Even her skin would grow rosier and younger looking. She did nothing different. She didn't take new medication, nor did she change her diet. Each day, she grew stronger. At her next medical checkup, her doctor was so astounded she called the other doctors to witness Sophie's miraculous recovery. They scratched their heads, theorized, and analyzed but could not find a scientifically sound reason for Sophie's healing. Sophie told them, "That's because the Black Madonna is beyond science!" Of course, most of them thought she was kooky, but Sophie didn't care. She was healed. She now makes it her duty to visit the Black Madonna's shrine regularly and share her story with anyone within earshot.

Fatima's Healing

Fatima had a loving relationship with her family. They had a lovely connection with one another, sharing their hopes and dreams, encouraging one another, and enjoying the love they had. Her childhood home was a safe haven, and there was never a moment when she would feel unloved or unheard. However, that would be ruined when a friend she'd invited to her home would tell her a malicious lie. It was a cruel lie. This "friend" of Fatima's had accused her brother, Ahmed, of abusing her. The lie was so vile it rocked the family to its core. The accusation was a grave one, so, of course, Fatima confronted her brother. The story was so horrific, and her friend was a master deceiver, so it was tough to believe Ahmed was innocent. The confrontation would become so intense that it utterly destroyed Fatima's connection with her loved ones. She believed her narcissistic friend so much that she felt duty-bound to stand by this person. Fatima's family was so angry and frustrated with her that they would eventually decide to oust her.

Fatima was shocked at being rejected by the people she called family. Not one person even bothered to call her after to learn how she was doing or where she had gone. She was angry. She was hurt. She was lonely. She thought she could count on her friend but would eventually discover one of this person's other lies. She had to cut ties with them at that point, so she felt truly alone. Weeks became months, months because years, and Fatima had grown used to being alone. She became distrustful and taught herself to live alone. She convinced herself she didn't need anyone and suppressed her loneliness. It was only a matter of time before Fatima's depression grew too much to bear.

One evening, tired of hiding in the small room of the tiny apartment she'd scrounged some money to rent, she decided to take a walk. The depressing and suicidal thoughts were becoming too much to bear, and she had learned taking walks was a good way to handle them. This evening, she felt compelled to take a different route than she was used to. So, she followed the urge. As she walked, she noticed a Black Madonna image beside a doorway. Curious, she stopped and stared at it, mesmerized. An old man opened the door and smiled at Fatima. "She wants to see you if you want to see her." He beckoned her in and walked ahead, not waiting to see if she followed him into the Black Madonna sanctuary. Fatima had a brief moment when she wanted to keep walking, but she thought to herself, "Well, if he's going to take my life, at least he'll put me out of my misery." She used to be such a bright, happy person, but now, thoughts like this had become the norm for her.

Fatima entered, and inside, she saw a statue of the Black Madonna. It was life-sized, but she felt it was larger than life. She was immediately drawn to the statue. As if in a trance, she walked toward the statue and began hitting it, screaming and crying. While she did that, it was as if no one else was in the room with her. It was only her and the Black Madonna. No one stopped her. She kept going, and eventually, she stopped hitting the statue and hugged it, and her screams died down to whimpers. "Please fix me. Please fix us." She repeated this simple prayer over and over. Eventually, she would fall asleep at the feet of the Black Virgin. Her hosts were warm and kind, and they took care of her until she left the next day. She felt lighter in her heart, and there was a pep in her step. The Black Mother had healed her. She showed Fatima that her family may have rejected her, but she had always been there. The Black Mother was her mother, father, brother, and sister. She was her friend and confidante.

Fatima practiced connecting with the Black Madonna daily, faithfully basking in her presence and receiving deep insights. She had wanted to reach out to her family, but the Mother told her there was no need. Six months after the evening at the Black Madonna sanctuary, her phone would ring. It was an unfamiliar number, and usually, Fatima made a point of avoiding calls from numbers she didn't recognize. As her phone rang this time, it felt like time froze still. It felt like a date with destiny to her, and it was. When she answered, the voice on the other end belonged to her father. They arranged to meet with the rest of the family. Needless to say, the reunion was intense and healing for all. Fatima got the chance to apologize to Ahmed, and her family apologized for abandoning her. In doing this, their emotional wounds were healed. The Black Mother fueled the forgiveness and understanding among them with her essence. Fatima's faith in the Mother is now stronger than ever.

Sophie's and Fatima's stories are only two of thousands upon thousands that demonstrate the divine healing power of the Black Madonna. There is no wound too deep for her to heal and no rift she cannot fix.

The Dark Mother's Nurturing Qualities

Would you like to know how the Dark Mother can care for you? Here's a close look at the Black Madonna's traits, specifically regarding her role as a nurturer, which is an expression of the Divine feminine.

She Offers Unconditional Love. The moment you decide to connect with the Divine Feminine, you'll find her love embracing you. The Dark

Mother is as tender as she is powerful. She doesn't need you to be or do anything special before she shows you her love. Look at Fatima, for instance. She made an honest mistake, but the African Mother didn't care. She didn't get angry at Fatima's way of expressing her pain and grief. She loved and still loves her, regardless. The Mother feels the same about you.

She Is Always Compassionate and Full of Empathy. She gets you. This isn't just some sentence to make you feel warm and fuzzy. The Dark Mother really does understand and empathize with you. More than anyone else, she knows the sorrows you experience. She feels your joy and your pain. So, whenever you feel challenged or feel as if life is too much, remember she's right with you. She's there to shoulder your burdens. If you need someone to listen without judgment, turn to her; she will offer you her ears and heart.

She Protects and Comforts You. In the middle of a storm, you can trust her with your worries and fears. You will feel your fears melt away as you realize the Divine Feminine within you is greater than anything that could come against you. You can take comfort in her loving embrace and allow that to fuel your heart with courage.

She Heals You and Renews Your Life. Whether you're dealing with a scraped knee or a battered heart, she will bring you healing. She is ease, flow, and rejuvenation. Her presence in your life keeps things fresh, making it impossible for any wound to fester and take you down.

She Gives You Strength. When you have a challenge or a struggle, you can count on her to fuel you with the fortitude you need to persevere. Just when you think you're all tapped out, she emerges as your second wind, helping you deal with your issues with uncommon grace.

Healing through Devotion

You can use prayer, healing rituals, sacred healing dance, and similar techniques to help you connect to the healing power of the Black Madonna.

The Power of Prayer

By praying, you can connect with the Black Madonna. Praying doesn't require special clothes or circumstances. It is inner work because you only need an open heart with clear intentions. Praying involves having a conversation with the Divine Feminine. You can share your feelings and thoughts with her or simply state your intentions and ask her to bless them. You can request healing, and she will answer you.

How: Before you start your day, take five to ten minutes to sit in silence and shut your eyes. After a few deep breaths, you may begin to speak with the Black Madonna. Tell her what you would like her to heal. Share your dreams and fears. She is a confidante, so you can tell her everything and anything. When you're done, sit in silence and wait for any insights. You may also sit in silence until you feel peace, which confirms you've been heard and your prayer is answered.

Healing Rituals

A ritual is a ceremony with a precise sequence of events and certain elements that make it special. Rituals can be elaborate or simple. You may light a candle, burn some incense, set up an altar and pray at it, or do all these and more. The idea is rituals cause the energy of the Black Madonna to come through stronger because you're being intentional in your desire to connect with her as you perform the ritual. The ritual can demonstrate your love for the Mother, and on top of that, it's a channel that allows her healing love to flow through you and to you.

How: Designate a small area of your home as a sacred space. If you have some sage, you can burn it to cleanse the energy of this space first. Get a picture or carving of the Black Madonna and place it in this space, on the floor, or on a table, which will become your dedicated altar. If you have any other items that remind you of the Black Madonna, you can set them with the statue or artwork, too. When preparing to perform a ritual, you should always start by cleansing the space with sage. Then, light a candle, sit with your eyes shut for a few moments, and take some deep breaths to center yourself. When you're relaxed and still, you can open your eyes and contemplate the Black Madonna. Or, keep your eyes shut and pray or meditate on her essence. When you have finished, always allow the candle to go out by itself, and thank her for honoring you with her presence. Please never leave a burning candle or incense unattended.

Sacred Healing Dance

Your body is intelligent. One of the ways it can express that intelligence is through dance. As you dance, you express yourself. Dancing with the intention of experiencing the Black Madonna's healing in your life will definitely draw that power to you. By engaging in sacred healing dances, you release the emotions that are pent up within you. You accept her solace and comfort, healing, guidance, and more.

How: Pick any music reminiscent of the essence of the Black Mother. It should uplift you spiritually, and it's best if it has no lyrics to distract you. Find somewhere private and peaceful in your home or a peaceful area outdoors. Allow your body to move. Think of the music as a question and your body's movements as the answer. You can turn your brain off by feeling your body as you move. Notice how different movements affect you. Allow your emotions to come out through your body however they want. This isn't for Broadway: this is to allow the Divine Mother's energy to flow through you so you can heal, so keep this intention front and center in your mind.

Chapter 9: Honoring the Mother Goddess

People honor the Black Madonna in various ways, whether alone or as a community. By understanding how people show their devotion to the Virgin, you, too, will know how you can show her your life and appreciation.

Altars and Shrines

All over the world, you can find shrines in the Black Madonna's honor. Public shrines are large enough to cater to many devotees at once. How do you set up your own altar? People set up altars in their homes to honor the Mother even when they're nowhere near a shrine. Well, first, you need to have a sacred space. As you set up your altar, you need to be intentional about it. Pick a space that feels right or somewhere meaningful to you and the others around you who are devoted to the Black Madonna. This is no ordinary space. It's a portal that will allow the Mother's energy to come through powerfully.

One main element of an altar or shrine is art. You need depictions of the Black Madonna, whether paintings, sculptures, or both. They are more than representations of the Divine Feminine; they are also portals allowing the Divine and the earthly to merge. Placing them in your shrine or on your altar gives everyone something to focus on as they pray, meditate, or contemplate.

You're also going to need candles. Now that you have the Virgin's presence in your heart, the candle's flame represents the inner divine light that shines within you. As you light a candle, you perform a ritual. You draw on the warm and loving energies of the Mother and make it easier for inner alchemy to occur within you as you remain at the altar or shrine. Since the Mother has a connection with nature, you may want to include flowers and foliage on the altar to honor this aspect of the Madonna. When you use fresh flowers, they represent the ideas of growth and inner beauty. As for greenery, that represents the fertility of the Divine Mother and her ability to renew you and bless you abundantly.

If you wish, you can add other items that mean something to you or your community and connect you to the Black Virgin. You may feel inspired to add seashells, special stones and crystals, water vessels, and even drawn or carved symbols to draw even more of her energy to the altar or shine. When you have set up your altar, you can make offerings to her. Your offering could be as simple as a glass of water. It could take more work, like a well-prepared meal. You could offer other items that are dear to you. It doesn't matter what you offer as long as you're intuitively led to offer that item, and you do so with a true sense of appreciation for the Black Mother. When you're not busy appreciating her at the altar or shrine, you may simply contemplate her essence or reflect on the insights she has given you.

Candlelight Vigils

It's the light of the soul and the light of the Divine Feminine who nurtures you and keeps you safe and warm.

LatakiaHill, CC BY-SA 4.0 <https://creativecommons.org/licenses/by-sa/4.0>, via Wikimedia Commons: https://commons.wikimedia.org/wiki/File:Candlelight_Vigil_at_University_of_Chicago_for_Urumchi_Fire.jpg

Devotees of the Black Virgin also have candlelight vigils in her honor. These are no ordinary rituals. They are meant to revere her and to unite everyone in her love. Each flame represents the inner light of divinity each devotee has within them. It's the light of the soul and the light of the Divine Feminine who nurtures you and keeps you safe and warm. Candlelight vigils are excellent for unifying communities. The energy of warmth and solidarity is palpable. Everyone stands together, staring intently into the candle flame in their hand. If you ever get the chance to be part of a vigil, you should go. You'll be glad you attended.

Festivals and Pilgrimages

People honor and celebrate the Black Virgin through festivals and by making pilgrimages. Pilgrimages are trips to sacred sites and often have people from all over the world participating. The festivals are full of joy and light; everyone is fully aware of their spiritual nature and connection to others and the Divine. You can find these festivals wherever shrines or sites are dedicated to the Black Virgin. For instance, there is the Madonna of Altötting. Each year, at least one million faithful make their way to Altötting to thank her and pray for her miracles and blessings at Our Lady Altötting, which is in the Chapel of Mercy or Gnadenkapelle (Chapel of Mercy). You may also enjoy the Sara Gypsy Festival, which is held in the Camargue. Expect to meet gypsies by the thousands at this festival as they come to honor the Black Madonna.

Festivals and pilgrimages are excellent for cultural expression and communing with like-minded people. You experience a spiritual connection unlike anything else when you partake in them. There are ceremonies and rituals, prayers, processions, and more. Also, there are always miracles and testimonies. The spiritual importance of the Black Virgin's sites and shrines cannot be overstated. They offer physical points of contact for those who know the Mother and those who don't to experience her powerfully. Typically, the sites are serene places with interesting histories and incorporate elements of nature. When you take a trip to these places, you can consider your journey a metaphor for your inner alchemical journey. The following is a list of annual holy days and feast days in honor of the Black Madonna and their locations. Remember that the dates may vary depending on what's going on in the location, and there may be alterations to the liturgical calendars. Also, this is not an exhaustive list.

1. **Feast of Our Lady of Częstochowa:** August 26th, at the Jasna Góra Monastery, Częstochowa, Poland.
2. **Feast of Our Lady of Lourdes:** February 11th, at the Sanctuary of Our Lady of Lourdes, Lourdes, France.
3. **Feast of Our Lady of Montserrat:** April 27th, at the Montserrat Monastery, Catalonia, Spain.
4. **Feast of Our Lady of Prompt Succor:** January 8th, at the National Shrine of Our Lady of Prompt Succor, New Orleans, Louisiana, United States of America.
5. **Feast of Our Lady of Guadalupe:** December 12th, at the Basilica of Our Lady of Guadalupe, Mexico City, Mexico.
6. **Feast of Our Lady of Regla:** September 8th, at the Basilica of Nuestra Señora de Regla, Regla, Cuba.
7. **Feast of Our Lady of Montevergine:** February 2nd, at the Abbey of Montevergine, Naples, Southern Italy. (This event is dear to the LGBT community, as the Madonna of Montevergine has historically been of help to them, going as far back as medieval times.)
8. **Feast of Our Lady of Einsiedeln:** September 14th, at the Einsiedeln Abbey, Einsiedeln, Switzerland.
9. **Feast of our Lady of Candelaria:** February 2nd, at the Basilica of Candelaria, Tenerife, Canary Islands, Spain.
10. **Feast of Our Lady of Altötting:** September 12th, at the Chapel of Grace, Altötting, Germany.
11. **Feast of Our Lady of Tindari:** September 8th, at the Sanctuary of Tindari, Sicily, Italy.
12. **Feast of Our Lady of Walsingham:** September 24th, at the Shrine of Our Lady of Walsingham, Norfolk, England.
13. **Feast of Our Lady of Africa:** April 20th, at the Notre Dame d'Afrique, Algiers, Algeria.
14. **Feast of Mary, Divine Mother (Solemnity of Mary, Mother of God):** January 1st, at Catholic Churches worldwide.

Meditation and Contemplation

Black Madonna devotees recognize the importance of the twin practices of meditation and contemplation because they make it easier to connect with the energy of the Divine Feminine and keep it flowing in their lives. They realize that the Black Madonna's guidance becomes clearer when they spend time doing these things. Meditation is about keeping your attention on one thing, whether an object, your breath, or a mantra or affirmation, to help you become more mindful of the moment and in general.

On the other hand, contemplation involves bringing a specific interest or concern to mind, sitting with it mindfully, exploring every aspect of it that you can, and coming up with profound insights on the subject. You may contemplate the Black Madonna, an aspect of her being, a symbol, or anything else you desire.

You already know how to meditate. Now, the question is, how do you contemplate? Specifically, how do you contemplate the Black Madonna to honor her?

A good way to adjust the ambiance of the space would be to use one or more candles rather than daylight or even harsher electrical light.
https://www.pexels.com/photo/silhouette-of-person-raising-its-hand-268134/

Location: Pick a quiet and comfy spot, distraction-free and welcoming. You should enjoy being in this place. A good way to adjust the ambiance of the space would be to use one or more candles rather than daylight or even harsher electrical light. When you light incense, you make the atmosphere feel even more sacred. This is excellent for your contemplation.

Intention: Choose which aspect of the Madonna you would like to contemplate. Do you want to mine gold from the idea of integrating opposites? Would you like to make peace with darkness and see what gifts it has to offer you? Do you want to understand how to allow more of the Black Madonna's alchemical transformation or spiritual healing? Figure out your intention.

Whatever you have chosen, craft a short question that summarizes what you'd like to contemplate. For instance, you could ask, "How can I allow more ease in my life with the Black Madonna's help?" This will be your anchor question. You'll understand why you need it soon. If you like, you can also contemplate something physical, like her statue, picture, or anything you have that resonates with you and instantly reminds you of the Black Mother. If you wish, you may contemplate her eyes, skin, outstretched arms, or any element in her visual depiction to which you are drawn.

Contemplation: Contemplate whatever you've settled on. Shut your eyes, take a few deep breaths to anchor you to the here and now, and help you feel still and centered. When you notice the distinct peace that comes when you meditate, you may open your eyes and look at whatever you want to contemplate. If it's not visual, keep your eyes closed and allow your mind to explore your chosen subject.

Contemplation isn't something you force. You cannot rush the process, either. Take your time with this. If you can, do it at a time when you don't have any obligations so you're not subconsciously rushing yourself. Allow the thoughts and inner impressions to rise on their own within you. If you find you're wandering from your contemplation onto other thoughts, use your anchor question to bring you back. You may ask the question aloud, softly, or in your mind. This question will anchor you to the purpose of your contemplation.

You might have a new question as your mind lights up with insights. You can write that down to be the subject matter of your next contemplation if you need more time with the present matter. However, if you feel satisfied with what you have received so far and you still have time, you may contemplate the next thing. Note that it would be best to have a journal to make notes. If you find writing slow and tedious, use a recording app to speak your thoughts aloud and later transcribe them. It's always handy to have them in written form so you can read through them whenever you want or skip to particularly profound points from your contemplation that you'd like to ponder.

Integration: Now that you have received insight, it's time to make it useful. Why does that matter? You're not contemplating spiritual matters simply for the sake of knowledge. It's one thing to not know something and not act on it. After all, how can you act on information you don't have? It's another thing to have knowledge and do nothing with it or about it. Ground the wisdom you receive in practicality. Write or state at least three ways you can make it practical in your life. If it helps, consider each part of your life and come up with three things you'll do differently in each one, whether that's in your personal relationships, professional life, health, spiritual walk, and so on.

Conclusion: When you're done contemplating, you'll know it. It feels like being complete, for lack of a better way to describe it. When you arrive at this feeling, shut your eyes once more and thank the Black Madonna for her wisdom and guidance. Thank her in advance for helping you integrate the insights you've received from the contemplation into your daily life. You see, you have your inner will and determination, but those things can only get you so far. You'll have phenomenal results by asking and thanking her for the grace and strength to follow through on implementing what you've learned.

When you can't find it in you to do the right, wise thing, the Dark Virgin will step in and fuel you with the strength you need. You are expressing complete trust in her by thanking her right after your contemplation for helping with this. You're telling her you know she will help you with your mission of inner transformation. That sort of faith pleases her, and she'll be more than happy to prove you were right to trust her even before you had evidence of her help and blessing in your life.

Why Devotion Matters

You need to devote yourself to the Black Madonna to maintain your relationship with her. As you express this devotion, you'll be transformed in many ways and always for the better. By being deliberate about reaching out to her, you show her your love and nurture your bond with her. You also make it impossible for her blessings and healing not to flow to you. When you are devoted to the Divine Feminine, your spiritual life is set on fire, burning brighter, revealing more of your true self. You go beyond mere dogma and doctrine, as you have actual experiences of the divine. This is the benefit that devotion offers you.

Devotion is a way to allow yourself to heal on the inside, too. By deliberately bringing yourself to the Black Madonna's presence daily, you give her room to work on your wounds. She'll fix your traumas. She'll go through the past and mend what's broken in you. There's no better space to let her help with your emotional wounds than during devotion. Devotion is a service you offer the Black Madonna from your heart, from a place of truth and reverence. Some people think of her only when they need something, but they only shortchange themselves by doing this. With devotion, you come to her and relate with her as you would a friend. No one likes that one friend who only calls them when they need something. The Black Madonna is obviously not one to be phased by that, but it's only fair and right for you to make devotion a daily practice. As you do so, you'll experience more miracles and blessings. You'll gain more wisdom, and your spiritual development will soar.

By devoting yourself to the Dark Virgin, you build a bridge that takes you from mere head knowledge to heart knowledge of all spiritual matters. You're different from those who are talented at sounding like they know what they're talking about but don't have actual experiences with the Mother. You live her. You breathe her. She is as real to you as the words on this page. All that happens when you decide to devote yourself to her is to set up daily practices to remind yourself of her presence and benevolence in your life.

Devotion makes the ineffable tangible in your life. You will know, without a doubt, that there is more to life than your physical senses can pick up on. Devotion is like taking a daily drink from the eternally flowing river of life that is the Black Mother. It brings you peace. It helps you see beyond the illusions of the physical world, as it makes it easier for the Madonna to demonstrate her presence and remind you there's no one greater than her. So, when challenges, obstacles, and adversity rear their heads and seem insurmountable, you relax. You know, through devotion, you have a presence within you that is greater than anything the world could throw at you.

Conclusion

You now believe she is calling you, don't you? This book may have come to an end, but there is unfinished business between you and the Black Madonna. Something hangs in the air, waiting for you to dictate what happens next. Her invitation remains extended, her outstretched hands waiting, desiring you to reach out and take them with yours so she can show you the path to fulfillment, growth, freedom, and joy. You now know what her offer entails. You know what to expect from her and understand what is expected of you. Will you set this book down when you're done and continue about your business as if you can't see her asking you to let her make your life beautiful? Or will you take the leap, trusting that she will heal you on every level? Will you let her transform your life for the better? Will you accept her offer of peace and ease? Will you let her teach you what she knows so you can use the wisdom she offers to craft a life that aligns with your true self? You alone can answer that.

Through this book, you've been introduced to the enigma that is the Black Mother. You know how to recognize her presence. You feel a strong resonance with her, and this is no accident. You've discovered this benevolent force that can offer you spiritual transformation and show you the wonders and mysteries of the eternal Divine Feminine. You've learned how she blesses one and all and never discriminates in offering guidance, protection, and profound wisdom to those who seek her out and call upon her. You may have come to the conclusion of this book, but when it comes to your story with her, it remains incomplete. If you'd like to know how it goes, you have to trust her. Why not? There are so many reasons to accept her in your life.

The Dark Mother is resilience itself. She is a testament that you can endure the worst of the worst and still come out on top, transformed into the best version of yourself yet. That's the beauty of having a relationship with her. There's no cap on how much better things can get for you. She's in the business of leaving your jaw hanging with awe and gratitude as she takes you from height to height while you continue to honor her steadfastly in devotion. She's seen it all, from the rise and fall of kingdoms and empires to trials and triumphs that humanity has faced collectively and individually. She knows how ugly humanity can get, yet she is equally aware of your potential to thrive and soar. Your Divine Mother wants you to know your potential and to make it real.

If you say yes to her, be warned that you will never remain the same. Your transformation will be so brilliant and beautiful that you'll hardly be able to recognize the person you were before you read this book. The Black Madonna will show you she is not some far-off god who picks and chooses who gets their prayers answered. She will be a loving friend, mother, and guide, right by your side, steering you down the paths you should take. You may feel some regret about not having known her before now or wasting time waffling between whether or not you should surrender your life to her. However, don't waste your time this way. You are exactly where you should be. Moreover, you can rest knowing she doesn't care for calendars or clocks. The Black Madonna is never late.

Appendix: List of Black Madonnas

Our Lady of Consolation of the Dejected and Oppressed

Our Lady of Consolation of the Dejected and Oppressed.
SICDAMNOME, CC BY-SA 4.0 <https://creativecommons.org/licenses/by-sa/4.0>, via Wikimedia Commons: https://commons.wikimedia.org/wiki/File:Our_Lady_of_Consolation_Grinstead_Great_Britain.jpg

Our Lady of Kibeho

Our Lady of Kibeho.
https://commons.wikimedia.org/wiki/File:Our_Lady_of_Kibeho_-_Rosary_Team_-_Public_Domain.jpg

Our Lady of Deliverance

Our Lady of Deliverance.
Judgefloro, CC0, via Wikimedia Commons:
https://commons.wikimedia.org/wiki/File:8456Marian_Healing_Exhibit_with_Saints_18.jpg

Virgin Mary of Einsiedeln

Virgin Mary of Einsiedeln.
Martin Dürrschnabel, CC BY-SA 2.5 <https://creativecommons.org/licenses/by-sa/2.5>, via Wikimedia Commons: https://commons.wikimedia.org/wiki/File:Schwarze_Madonna.jpg

Our Lady of Guadalupe

Our Lady of Guadalupe.
https://commons.wikimedia.org/wiki/File:1531_Nuestra_Se%C3%B1ora_de_Guadalupe_anagoria.jpg

The Virgin of Juquila

The Virgin of Juquila.
Virgendelosremedios, CC BY-SA 4.0 <https://creativecommons.org/licenses/by-sa/4.0>, via Wikimedia Commons: https://commons.wikimedia.org/wiki/File:Coronada_Juquila.jpg

Our Lady of Loreto

Our Lady of Loreto.
Flyer20061, CC BY-SA 3.0 <https://creativecommons.org/licenses/by-sa/3.0>, via Wikimedia Commons: https://commons.wikimedia.org/wiki/File:Our_Lady_of_Loreto.jpg

Our Lady of Altötting

Our Lady of Altötting.
*S. Finner: Siddhartha Finner, Dipl.Ing.-Architektur, CC BY-SA 3.0
<https://creativecommons.org/licenses/by-sa/3.0>, via Wikimedia Commons:
https://commons.wikimedia.org/wiki/File:Gnadenbild,_Gnadenkapelle_Alt%C3%B6tting.jpeg*

Notre Dame de la Sarte

Notre Dame de la Sarte.
https://commons.wikimedia.org/wiki/File:Statue_Notre-Dame_de_La_Sarte.jpg

La Vierge Noire d'Outremeuse

La Vierge Noire d'Outremeuse.
See page for author, CC BY-SA 3.0 <http://creativecommons.org/licenses/by-sa/3.0/>, via Wikimedia Commons: https://commons.wikimedia.org/wiki/File:Procession_2006_-n%C2%B06.JPG

The Black Virgin

The Black Virgin.
https://commons.wikimedia.org/wiki/File:Black_virgin_of_russia.jpg

Marija Bistrica

Marija Bistrica.
No machine-readable author provided. Severus assumed (based on copyright claims). CC BY-SA 3.0 <http://creativecommons.org/licenses/by-sa/3.0/>, via Wikimedia Commons: https://commons.wikimedia.org/wiki/File:Marija_Bistrica.jpg

Nuestra Señora de la Caridad del Cobre

Nuestra Señora de la Caridad del Cobre.
*Hyppolyte de Saint-Rambert, CC BY-SA 4.0 <https://creativecommons.org/licenses/by-sa/4.0>,
via Wikimedia Commons:*
https://commons.wikimedia.org/wiki/File:Santiago_Virgen_de_La_Caridad_del_Cobre_hdsr_S5i s_Cuba2_841.jpg

The Eleousa of Kykkos

The Eleousa of Kykkos.
https://commons.wikimedia.org/wiki/File:Municipal_Gallery_of_Ioannina_-_Mother_of_God_Eleousa_of_Kykkos_1860.jpg

Here's another book by Mari Silva that you might like

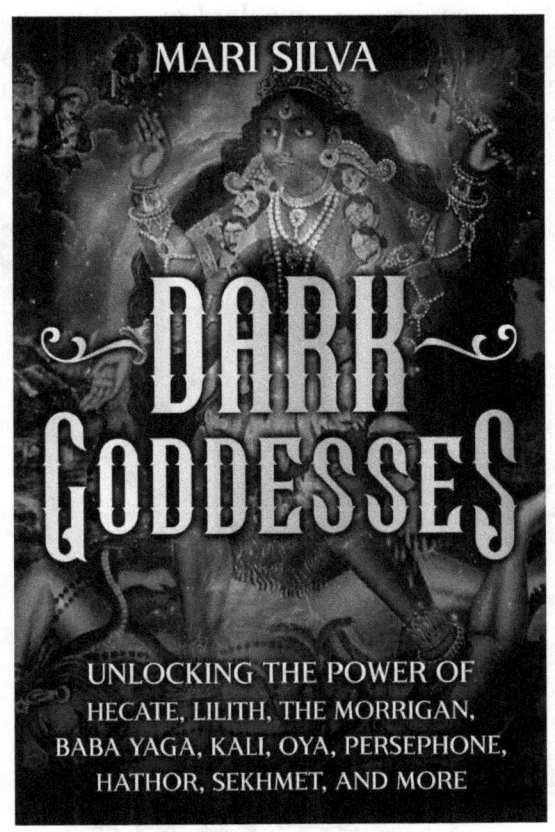

Your Free Gift
(only available for a limited time)

Thanks for getting this book! If you want to learn more about various spirituality topics, then join Mari Silva's community and get a free guided meditation MP3 for awakening your third eye. This guided meditation mp3 is designed to open and strengthen ones third eye so you can experience a higher state of consciousness. Simply visit the link below the image to get started.

https://spiritualityspot.com/meditation

Or, Scan the QR code!

References

Arain, N. (2017). Goddess Empowerment. Createspace Independent Publishing Platform.

Asavei, M. A., & Bushnell, A. M. (2022). Feminist spirituality and Roma artistic activism: the Afterlife of the uncanonised Saint Sara Kali. Identities, 1-18.

Begg, E. (2017). The Cult of the Black Virgin. Chiron Publications.

Belloni, A., & Fox, M. (2019). Healing journeys with the black madonna: chants, music, and sacred practices of the great goddess. Bear & Company.

Courtney Hall Lee. (2017). Black Madonna: a womanist look at Mary of Nazareth. Cascade Books, An Imprint Of Wipf And Stock Publishers.

Georgieff, S. (2016). The black madonna: mysterious soul companion / Stepanie Georgieff. Outskirts Press.

Grace, A. (2021). Divine Feminine Energy. Stonebank Publishing.

Gustafson, F. (2009). The Black Madonna of Einsiedeln. Daimon Verlag.

Małgorzata Oleszkiewicz-Peralba. (2007). The Black Madonna in Latin America and Europe.

Marsman, M. A. (2019). Kali: in praise of the goddess. Psychological perspectives.

Mato, T. (1994). The Black Madonna Within. Open Court Publishing.

Michello, J. (2020). The black madonna: A theoretical framework for the African origins of other world religious beliefs. Religions.

Price, I., & Judith, A. (2017). Goddess Power: Awakening the Wisdom of the Divine Feminine in Your Life. Mango Media.

Strand, C., & Lytle, W. (2022). Waking up to the dark: the Black Madonna's gospel for an age of extinction and collapse. Monkfish Book Publishing Company.

Stuckey, J. H. (2005). Ancient mother goddesses and fertility cults. Journal of the Motherhood Initiative for Research and Community Involvement

www.ingramcontent.com/pod-product-compliance
Lightning Source LLC
Chambersburg PA
CBHW072152200426
43209CB00052B/1149